双语背景下的运动事件认知
——以英汉学习者为例

Motion Event Cognition in Bilingual Mind:
A Study of Chinese-English Speakers

纪瑛琳◎著

中山大学出版社
·广州·

版权所有　翻印必究

图书在版编目（CIP）数据

双语背景下的运动事件认知：以英汉学习者为例＝Motion Event Cognition in Bilingual Mind：A Study of Chinese-English Speakers：英文／纪瑛琳著 . —广州：中山大学出版社，2022.2
 ISBN 978 – 7 – 306 – 07417 – 1

Ⅰ. ①双… Ⅱ. ①纪… Ⅲ. ①英语—对比语言学—对比研究—汉语 Ⅳ. ①H31 ②H1

中国版本图书馆 CIP 数据核字（2022）第 026057 号

SHUANGYU BEIJING XIA DE YUNDONG SHIJIAN RENZHI

出 版 人：王天琪
策划编辑：熊锡源
责任编辑：熊锡源
封面设计：林绵华
责任校对：李昭莹
责任技编：靳晓虹
出版发行：中山大学出版社
电　　话：编辑部 020 – 84110283，84113349，84111997，84110779，84110776
　　　　　 发行部 020 – 84111998，84111981，84111160
地　　址：广州市新港西路 135 号
邮　　编：510275　　传　　真：020 – 84036565
网　　址：http：//www.zsup.com.cn　E-mail：zdcbs@mail.sysu.edu.cn
印　刷　者：广州市友盛彩印有限公司
规　　格：880mm×1230mm　1/32　4.75 印张　150 千字
版次印次：2022 年 2 月第 1 版　2022 年 2 月第 1 次印刷
定　　价：30.00 元

如发现本书因印装质量影响阅读，请与出版社发行部联系调换

国家社科基金项目"英汉语学习者运动事件的心理呈现"(15BYY063)研究成果

For Jerry

Acknowledgements

This book has stemmed from a research report I completed for a scientific project funded by the National Social Science Fund of China (NSSFC, project code: 15BYY063). I am very grateful to the three anonymous reviewers of the report who read the earliest version of this book and offered insightful suggestions for revision.

Several chapters of this book have been published in the form of journal articles. An adapted version of Chapter 4, together with some parts of Chapter 3, titled "Cognitive Representation of Spontaneous Motion in a Second Language: An Exploration of Chinese Learners of English", was published in *Frontiers in Psychology — Cognition*, doi: 10.3389/fpsyg.2019.02706 (Copyright 2019 by Frontiers Media S. A., Bern, Switzerland). A slightly different version of Chapter 5, along with some parts of Chapter 3, titled "Motion Event Similarity Judgments in One or Two Languages: An Exploration of Monolingual Speakers of English and Chinese vs. L2 Learners of English", has appeared in *Frontiers in Psychology — Language Sciences*, doi: 10.3389/fpsyg.2017.00909 (Copyright 2017 by Frontiers Media S. A., Bern, Switzerland). A Chinese version of the "Results" part of Chapter 6, titled "The Conceptualisation of Motion Events by English-Chinese Bilinguals: Evidence from Behavioural Tasks", has been published in *Modern Foreign Languages* 43 (5), 667-679 (Copyright 2020 by Guangdong University of Foreign Studies, Guangzhou, China). I am grateful to editors and publishers for their permission to reprint. Finally, an extended Chinese version of Section 2.1, Chapter 2, appears in *The Journal of*

Shenzhen University (Humanities and Social Sciences Edition [2021]).

As regards financial support, I am deeply indebted to NSSFC for generously funding the empirical studies reported in this book. I also owe my sincere gratitude to Shenzhen University Social Sciences Foundation from which I received continuous support in the past several years in my work.

I would like to say a big thank you to all participants and student assistants in my experiments. Their cheerful participation and cooperation makes the publication of this book possible. It is worth mentioning that this book was completed in a turbulent and stressful period of my personal life. My beloved son Jerry stood by me through that hard time with his unconditional love and trust. I dedicate this book to him.

Table of Contents

List of Figures ··· i

List of Tables ··· ii

Chapter 1　Introduction: Representing Motion Events Within and Beyond Language ···································· 1

Chapter 2　Narrating Motion Events in an L2—Evidence from English and Korean Learners of Chinese ········ 13

　　2.1　How English learners across proficiencies acquire motion expressions in Chinese: A review of study by Ji (2021) ·· 17

　　2.2　How Korean learners across proficiencies acquire motion expressions in Chinese: A review of study by Jin (2020) ·· 27

Chapter 3　Motion Event Cognition in Bilingual Speakers ·· 35

　　3.1　Representing motion events in an L2 context ·· 35

　　3.2　Manner-salience in English and Manner- and

I

Path-salience in Chinese 37
3.3 Motion event cognition in L2 learners 42

Chapter 4 The Conceptualisation of Voluntary Motion Events in L2 English Learners (Experiment 1) 48
4.1 Predictions 48
4.2 Methodology 51
    4.2.1 Participants 51
    4.2.2 Materials 54
    4.2.3 Pretest 55
    4.2.4 Testing session 56
    4.2.5 Coding 58
4.3 Results 59
    4.3.1 Mean number of Manner-matches and Path-matches across 5 participant groups 60
    4.3.2 RT in judgment across 5 groups of participants 63
4.4 Discussion 65

Chapter 5 The Conceptualisation of Caused Motion Events in L2 English Learners (Experiment 2) 73
5.1 Research questions and hypotheses 74
5.2 Materials 77
5.3 Results 78
    5.3.1 Number of Manner- and Path-matched judgments across 5 participant groups 79

  5.3.2 RT in Manner- and Path-matched judgments across 5 participant groups ········ 82
  5.4 Discussion ········ 85

Chapter 6 **Conceptualising Motion Events in L2 Chinese Learners (Experiments 3)** ········ 92
  6.1 Research methodologies ········ 94
  6.2 Results ········ 95
    6.2.1 Mean proportion of Manner-matches and Path-matches across 4 participant groups ········ 95
    6.2.2 The proportion of Path-matches across stimulus items ········ 98
    6.2.3 RT across 4 participant groups ········ 100
  6.3 Discussion of the results ········ 103

Chapter 7 **General Remarks** ········ 107
  7.1 Significance of the study ········ 109
  7.2 Directions for future research ········ 111

References ········ 114

Appendices ········ 128

List of Figures

Chapter 4

Figure 1 Mean number of Manner- and Path-matches across 5 participant groups

Figure 2 Mean RT (in ms) to Manner- and Path-matches across participant groups

Chapter 5

Figure 3 Mean number of Manner-matched and Path-matched preferences across 5 participant groups

Figure 4 The mean RT (in ms) to Manner- vs. Path-matches across participant groups

Chapter 6

Figure 5 Mean proportion of Path-matches and Manner-matches across 4 groups

Figure 6 Mean proportion of Path-matches by participant group and test item

Figure 7 The mean RT (in ms) to Manner- and Path-matches across participant groups

List of Tables

Chapter 4
Table 1   Groups of participants in the study
Table 2   Mean numbers of Manner- vs. Path-matches in 5 participant groups
Table 3   Regression coefficients for the logistic regression mixed model for Path-matches
Table 4   Mean RT (in ms) to spontaneous motion scenes in 5 participant groups
Table 5   Regression coefficients for the mixed model for RT to all items

Chapter 5
Table 6   RT (in ms) in Manner-matched and Path-matched conditions across participant groups

Chapter 6
Table 7   Mean RT (in ms) to stimulus motion scenes in 4 participant groups

Chapter 1
Introduction: Representing Motion Events Within and Beyond Language

In his Representational Modularity Hypothesis, Jackendoff (1999) raises three key questions regarding the interface between spatial language and nonlinguistic spatial thought, viz., how does the mind or brain encode spatial information (mainly visual), how does it encode linguistic information, and how does it communicate between the two (1999: 1)? Using different patterns of language to reflect our visual perception of spatial events and configurations and further understanding these events and relationships in a framework laid by one's native language has thus interested researchers from varied lines of scientific investigation such as linguists, psychologists, philosophers and neurologists.

The reason why the domain of space, motion event in particular, has attracted the attention of a considerable number of researchers is pretty obvious. The spatial event is so pervasive in our daily life that the conversion about the whereabouts of a given entity and the movement of human beings between and among different locations constitute a predominating percentage of our speech activities. The most intriguing point at the interface of language and space is a seemingly paradoxical observation. Our perception of visual events involves processes of 'converting retinal information into visual information, including some sort of retinotopic mapping' (Jackendoff, 1999: 1). To put it another way, this is a biologically determined process and believed to be universal among human beings. Strangely, such universality in perception (and presumably in cognition) is not reflected in the system of languages. In fact, world languages show a tendency to recruit quite different patterns to describe the same event. Slobin's (2004) *"Frog, Where Are You?"* study offers a case in point. When requested to orally describe a scene which depicts an owl popping out of a tree hole suddenly, participants from varied language backgrounds are found to systematically differ in what semantic component(s) they have chosen to encode in the verb, as demonstrated, below (2004: 6).

1. a. Spanish: *Sale un buho.* (=Exits an owl.)
   b. French: *D'un trou de l'arbre sort un hibou.*
      (=From a hole of the tree exits an owl.)
   c. Italian: *Da quest'albero esce un gufo.* (=From that tree exits an owl.)
   d. Turkish: *Oradan bir baykuşçı kıyor.* (=From there an owl exits.)
   e. Hebrew: *Yaca mitox haxor yanšuf.* (=Exits from:inside the:hole owl.)
2. a. English: *An owl popped out.*
   b. German: ... *weil da eine Eule plötzlich raus-flattert.*
      (=...because there an owl suddenly out-flaps)
   c. Dutch: ... *omdat er een uil uit-vliegt.* (=... because there an owl out-flies)
   d. Russian: *Tam vy-skočila sova.* (=There out-jumped owl.)
   e. Mandarin: *Fei 1 chu 1 yi 1 zhi 1 mao 1 tou 2 ying 1.*

Chapter 1   Introduction: Representing Motion Events Within and Beyond Language

(=Fly out one owl.)

In example 1, speakers of Spanish, French and Italian (mostly Romance languages) tend to denote the path of movement (i.e. *exit*) in the main verb, whereas in example 2, speakers of English, German and Dutch (mostly Germanic languages) have chosen to encode manner of movement (e.g. *fly*, *pop*, *flap*) in the verb. The two groups of participants look at the same picture, yet they tell quite different aspects of the same story: the former attends to the trajectory of motion, that is, how the bird moves from being 'within the hole' to being 'out of the hole' (i.e. boundary-crossing). In stark contrast, the latter pays particular attention to how the owl gets out of the hole: its speed, its suddenness, its wingspan, and so on (i.e. motor pattern).

Such an observation echoes with the gist of Talmy's (1985) motion event typology in which he claims that most Germanic languages, as exemplified by English and German, belong to satellite-framed languages which encode Manner of motion in the verb root whilst expressing Path of motion in verb supporting elements such as particles and prepositions. Meanwhile, as represented by Spanish and French, most Romance languages form verb-framed languages which tend to put Path of motion in the main verb of a sentence and Manner of motion in subordinated clauses, gerundives or even nouns, viz., out of the main verb (e.g. *skater*, *runner*, *skier*, *sailor*).

Not all languages fit neatly with the above system of classification. Chinese, for instance, poses a challenge for this bipartite category. As will be detailed in Chapter 2, this language characteristically uses a compound verb (e.g. *pa* 2-*shang* 4 'climb-up/ ascend') to describe motion events. Each component in it possesses independent syntactic function, and thus all components are believed to have equal formal significance. Slobin (2004) thus terms it 'an equipollently-framed language'. Talmy (2009) acknowledges that Chinese is not exactly like English and is not fully and completely satellite-framed as he originally proposed; it seems to be a language with 'two systems' (i.e. both satellite-framed and verb-framed). Similarly, Ji (2014) considers Chinese as standing midway along a verb-framed and satellite-framed continuum.

Observations as such lead to a considerable number of studies looking into typological features of world languages (and dialects) in motion event description. These studies reveal interesting intra-typological differences as well as widely attested inter-typological variations (see, for instance, Berthele, 2004; Brown, 2004; Choi & Bowerman, 1991; Croft *et al.*, 2002; Hendriks *et al.*, 2008; Iacobini & Masini, 2006; Li, 1990; Tai, 2003; Talmy, 1991; Zlatev & David, 2004). This line of inquiry goes further to examine how children acquire the standard pattern of motion description in their respective languages. Do they go through similar stages in their progression? Do they fully acquire the typical motion expressions in their native language with similar speed and at similar point of time? Most importantly, which force plays a larger role in driving their acquisition, cognitive universal mechanism or language-specific factors? Generally speaking, such investigations reveal, at least partially, a strong influence of language-specific features in children's acquisition of motion event expressions (and their encoding of static locations), which not only challenges the Piagetian tradition (Piaget & Inhelder, 1956) in acquisitional studies, but also leads to a new respect for the driving strength of specific languages in acquisitional progression (Bowerman, 1988, 1994, 1996; Bowerman & Choi, 2001, 2003; Clark, 1973; Farwell, 1977; Gullberg *et al.*, 2008; Hickmann, 2003, 2006; Johnston, 1988; Johnston & Slobin, 1979; Landau &

Chapter 1   Introduction: Representing Motion Events Within and Beyond Language

Zukowski, 2003; Pruden *et al.*, 2004).

Some researchers extend the topic of acquisition to the field of second language (L2) learners (adult learners in particular). Compared with the vast bulk of literature on how children acquire spatial expressions, the research focusing on an L2 context is rather limited and in great need of expansion, particularly those involving non-Indo-European languages and languages with a dual system in motion event typology (e.g. Chinese). Such an extension links together, to a large extent, linguistics and psychology. Different from the traditional practice highlighting error analysis in L2 acquisition, researchers in the field of L2 motion expressions are more interested in another question, viz., what elements on earth have been acquired by adult learners, merely linguistic categories on the surface level or patterns of thought at a deeper level of conceptualisation? To what extent an L2 learner can acquire a new way of thinking whilst learning how to encode motion events in another language—How difficult (or less challenging) this process might be? Questions as such penetrate into the level of psychology and result in a revival of Whorfian hypothesis (or linguistic relativity hypothesis).

A considerable number of studies along this line of research produce linguistic, psychological and behavioural evidence in (at least partial) support of a Whorfian effect (e.g. Cadierno, 2008, 2010; Cadierno & Ruiz, 2006; Chen & Ai, 2009; Hendriks & Hickmann, 2011; Hendriks *et al.*, 2008; Marotta & Meini, 2012; Navarro & Nicoladis, 2005; Talmy, 2009; Vidakovic, 2012). Except for a few studies showing that L2 learners (from two typologically close languages) can generally shake off the constraints of their native language or first language (L1) influence and virtually fully acquire the lexicalisation pattern of motion events in an L2, most studies suggest that the acquisitional process for an adult L2 learner is rather challenging and the learning of grammatical categories seems to be accompanied by a switch (or an integration) of thinking patterns. This is most evident from the use of inter-language by L2 learners, and from the acquisitional difficulties they encounter in acquiring syntactic constructions and discourse strategies for L2 motion texts. The views of Slobin (1996: 80-89) are representative of this line of observation. He thinks that there is a specific way of thinking that is closely tied with one's native language, a thinking pattern that has been fostered in language-involved activities such as listening, speaking, reading, writing, translating, or even paralinguistic gestures. This particular way of thinking fits in well with a specific language and can be easily encoded in that language (e.g. accessibility of abundant lexicon, less effort in recruiting relevant grammatical categories). Once in shape, this thinking pattern, which is perfectly matched with one's native language, is rather hard to be restructured, reoriented, reintegrated or switched in one's adulthood. This explains, at least partially, why adult L2 learners generally have difficulties in fully and completely acquiring typical motion expressions in the target language, and showing traces from their first language (L1) influence from time to time.

  The discussion centering around spatial language and spatial thinking quickly goes beyond the linguistic level. A growing number of psycholinguists and neurolinguists are keen to know whether one's habitual language use can affect one's thinking mode. Due to the emergence of new technologies, studies along this line of inquiry utilize psychological and behavioural schemes and employ some quite advanced techniques such as eye tracking, ERP (event-related potentials) and fMRI (functional magnetic resonance imaging). Conclusions drawn from these studies show great divergence regarding the effect of language on mind, and reasons for this can be

Chapter 1   Introduction: Representing Motion Events Within and Beyond Language

varied: typological distance between languages under examination, presence or absence of shadowing tasks, nature of motion stimuli used, and so on (Bohnemeyer *et al.*, 2004; Fernald, 2008; Ji, 2017, 2019; Papafragou, 2008; Soroli & Hickmann, 2010; von Stutterheim *et al.*, 2012). Just like the topic of acquisition of spatial language in an L2 context, the discussion of motion event cognition in L2 learners soon becomes a new undertaking in the field of language, space and mind. As will be seen in the elaboration in the following chapters, this new line of research triggers an intense debate regarding linguistic relativity hypothesis and the relationship between language and thought in general.

As is shown in the above summary, the study of language (patterns of expression in particular), space (motion events in particular) and mind (patterns of thinking in particular) involves at least four domains: language typology, children's L1 acquisition, adults' L2 acquisition and the motion event cognition in L1 and L2 speakers. Very few researchers have conducted systematic investigations involving all these domains. A series of studies by Ji (2014, 2017, 2019) and her colleagues (Ji *et al.*, 2011a, 2011b, 2011c; Ji & Hohenstein, 2014a, 2014b) in the past ten years constitute an exception. Their studies reveal, at the interface of spatial language and spatial event cognition, the complex nature of the relationship between habitual language use and patterns of thinking and behaviour.

To start with, Ji *et al.* (2011a, 2011b, 2011c) examine adults' motion event expressions by Chinese and English speakers in an experiment in which college students are asked to narrate animated motion scenes illustrating both voluntary and caused motion events (e.g. *A cat climbs up the tree*; *A girl cycled across the railway tracks*). The results show that the typological status of Chinese seems to be quite flexible: it shows clear satellite-framed features in the expression of voluntary motion events, whilst verb-framed characteristics in encoding caused motion events. Based on evidence as such, the authors propose that Chinese has a 'parallel' system in which both verb-framed and satellite-framed structures are available in equally frequent contexts. They further examine whether, and how, language-specific factors influence the rate and the progression of children's acquisition of motion expressions. Specifically, they investigate the encoding of varied types of motion events in Chinese children at ages 3, 4, 5, 6, 8, 10 and adults, and then compare them with motion descriptions in age-matched English children. The results suggest some universal cognitive influences in the first instance, that is, the number of semantic components encoded in an utterance increases with age in both English and Chinese. There is also a developmental progression in utterance density in caused motion expressions at all ages. Meanwhile, language-specific differences have an equally important influence. In both contexts of voluntary and caused motion events, the semantic density of utterances is significantly higher in Chinese than in English between the ages of 3 and 8. The authors believe that such a significant difference may be resulted from the linguistic device used to encode motion events in Chinese, i.e. a verb compound which greatly facilitates the simultaneous encoding of varied motion ingredients.

Given that previous studies reveal that linguistic representation of space by native speakers shows striking typological differences and language-specific categories further influence adults' spatial reasoning at a deeper cognitive level, the authors extend the research on space and cognition by focusing on: a) whether children's spatial reasoning develops with their acquisition of spatial language (Ji & Hohenstein, 2018), and b) whether spatial expressions of bilingual learners reflect

Chapter 1 Introduction: Representing Motion Events Within and Beyond Language

language-specific modes of spatial conceptualisation (Ji & Hohenstein, 2014a, 2014b).

As far as topic a) is concerned, previous studies of language influence on spatial conceptualisation tend to focus on languages with opposing typological properties (satellite-framed vs. verb-framed). The proposed line of investigation extends the research to Chinese which shows both satellite-framed and verb-framed properties and presents a 'new' third type of 'equipollent' language in motion event typology (Slobin, 2004). Thus such a study involves languages showing less dramatic differences (equipollently-framed Chinese and satellite-framed English), which will reveal whether effects of language are strong enough to lead to variations in mental representation of space even with minimal differences between languages. Further, the majority of studies on spatial cognition are conducted with adults only (Levinson, 2003). One criticism of such studies is that any differences between groups could be due to culture rather than language. In this context, a study along line a) provides a rigorous test of linguistic influence on cognition by involving different aged children to tie language acquisition to cognitive development. Given that previous research has shown some link between children's cognition and language acquisition in verb-framed and satellite-framed languages (Hohenstein, 2005), it remains to be seen whether similar links would be evident in young learners of a serial verb language like Chinese. As such, the authors aim to determine whether a developmental pattern in acquisition of spatial language (as attested in Ji *et al.*, 2011a, 2011b, 2011c) manifests itself in children's spatial cognition. Specifically, they investigate language-specific influence on mental representation of motion events by examining different aged learners of Chinese in comparison with learners of English, and focus on two questions: 1) how does conceptualisation of motion events (change-of-location type) vary between speakers of Chinese and English? and 2) how does motion event conceptualisation change across ages? Such a study provides a direct test of the linguistic relativity hypothesis (Whorf, 1956). Using the scheme of preferential looking and measured by reaction time in millisecond (ms), their results indicate that children's cognition is similar prior to becoming accustomed to using the spatial language in ways typical to their native language but then shows differences after such habitual use. In other words, they reveal that language-specific categories shape the way we mentally represent motion events.

As regards topic b), given that earlier studies have shown variations in mental representation of spatial events among bilingual learners of satellite-framed and verb-framed languages (Hohenstein *et al.*, 2006), the authors (Ji & Hohenstein, 2014a, 2014b) aim to extend the research along this line to serial verb languages like Chinese. The rationale of such a bilingual study is that if language-specific differences are only superficial and can be easily ignored once another language is spoken, then reorganisation of spatial information in a second language should be less problematic. However, if spatial conceptualisation is constrained by specific properties of a given language and speaking a different language implies a new way of conceptualising motion events, then bilingual learners will have difficulty in fully adapting to target spatial language patterns. Their analyses focus on two questions: 1) how do motion expressions of Chinese/English adult bilinguals vary across proficiency levels within each L2 group? and 2) how do motion expressions of Chinese/English bilinguals differ from those of monolinguals at a given proficiency level? In this production task the adult speakers of Chinese and English are asked to describe cartoons showing change-of-location motion events to an imaginary interlocutor, and the results show that

Chapter 1   Introduction: Representing Motion Events Within and Beyond Language

although the spatial expressions of advanced bilingual speakers are very much like those of monolinguals, the performance of learners at low and intermediate levels still differs from that of monolinguals in ways that suggest influences from source and/or target languages. These findings indicate the possibility that language-specific differences are not superficial; learning a different language implies a new way of spatial conceptualisation.

Following the above-mentioned lines of research, this book seeks to further extend the research of language, space and mind to the realm of L2 motion event cognition, and to examine whether, and how, L2 learners can reorient and restructure their patterns of thinking and behaviour as a result of additional language learning. The outline of the book is as follows: The first chapter introduces the study of language and thought as reflected in the particular field of space and reviews main findings of previous research in domains such as motion event typology, first and second language acquisition of motion expressions, and motion event conceptualisation. Before going into the field of L2 cognition of motion events, two particular studies are reviewed to demonstrate how L2 learners acquire verbal expressions of motion events in a new language with the findings discussed in the context of the relationship between language and cognition in general (Chapter 2). The third chapter illustrates the rationale of studies for L2 motion event cognition and systematically reviews previous literature on the relevant topic. Chapter 4 and Chapter 5 report, respectively, how Chinese learners of English make similarity judgments of motion scenes, and to what extent their preferences in selection can be associated with the typological status of their source and/or target languages. Research methodologies including participants, stimuli and experimental procedures are expounded and results of data analyses are reported with their implications discussed in detail in association with linguistic relativity hypothesis and the relationship between language and thought in general. Chapter 6 looks at another type of L2 learners, i.e. English learners of Chinese who are switching from a lucid pattern of motion expressions (in English) to a rather complicated system of event encoding (in Chinese), and are experiencing a conceptual shift as reflected in their decision strategies in similarity judgments. The concluding chapter (Chapter 7) summarizes main findings of the three nonlinguistic experiments reported in this book, highlights the significance of the study and points out directions for future research.

Chapter 2
Narrating Motion Events in an L2— Evidence from English and Korean Learners of Chinese

Before we delve into the topic of motion event cognition by bilingual speakers, it is worthwhile to take a close look at how second language (L2) learners of Chinese linguistically express typical motion scenes. In the previous chapter, we very briefly review how English/Chinese bilinguals encode caused motion scenarios in an L2 with the results showing considerable constraints from the source language, particularly in learners of low proficiencies. In the following, we will review, in detail, two recent studies investigating how learners of a satellite-framed language (i.e. English) and a verb-framed language (i.e. Korean), respectively, acquire characteristic motion expressions in an equipollently-framed language (i.e. Chinese). These two studies utilize experimental stimuli and procedures closely similar to those in studies of motion event cognition, which will be elaborated on in the subsequent chapters. Seen this way, the specific findings in these two studies will provide an important insight, or even partially predict, the results of investigations of motion event conceptualisation. The logic behind is closely associated with the linguistic relativity hypothesis and can be roughly described as follows: if a given language, with its specific grammatical categories and distinctions, can shape the way its speakers linguistically describe given scenes, and on the basis of which, further shapes the way its speakers perceive and conceptualize given scenes, then for bilinguals, learning a second language entails acquiring an additional way of thinking. More importantly, such an influence will most probably go deeper into the level of mental conceptualisation and affect how bilingual speakers behave in varied cognitive tasks such as similarity judgments, objects categorisation and memory recall tests.

The reasons that the following two studies are selected for a detailed review are multiple. First of all, these two studies focus on voluntary or spontaneous motion events, which typically demonstrate how a protagonist moves in a specific manner and along a specific path. This type of motion events normally includes four semantic components, viz., manner of motion, path of motion, the concept of motion *per se*, and ground of motion (Talmy, 1985). It is believed to be most representative of varied types of motion events. To illustrate, a specific type of caused motion events involves accompanied movement on the part of the protagonist, i. e., the protagonist performs a specific action, which causes an object to move in a specific manner and along a specific path whilst the protagonist moving with the object throughout a given path (see the caused motion model in Hickman *et al.*, 2009; e.g. *A boy pushed a big balloon across the street, and himself walked across the street with the balloon at the same time*). This type of caused motion events presents a rather complex set of semantic components. Take the dimension of 'manner' as an example: we have the moving manner of the protagonist (i.e. *walking*), the moving manner of the object (i.e. *rolling*) and the specific manner in which the object has been provoked (i. e. *pushing*), etc. This makes the illustrated caused motion model present multiple events such as the causing event, the motion event and the event of simultaneity (i.e. the protagonist and the object moving at the same time).

One consequence of such a design is that at least part of the narrator's attention is devoted to the expression of given events that bear virtually no relationship with the concept of motion (e.g. simultaneity between multiple events). In experiments highlighting the communicative nature of the task (e.g. instructions such as 'to describe these motion events as fully as possible to an imaginary audience'), the participants may opt to produce some 'atypical' syntactic structure to achieve the communicative goal of the task whilst sacrificing the constructional brevity. Some previous studies have revealed that Chinese participants tend to use complex sentences involving subordination (e.g. *The boy walked down the hill whilst pulling a bag after him*), rather than simplex constructions (e.g. *The boy pulled a bag down the hill*), to encode caused motion events with accompanied movement in order to give as much information as possible to the unseen listener (e.g. Ji *et al.*, 2011a). By this it is meant that responses elicited using such a caused motion model may not be sufficiently representative: they may not represent the most typical way that speakers encode a motion event in a default context. In contrast, a simplex model of voluntary motion events includes a reasonable number of motion components and presents manner and path as equally salient and occurring at the same time, thus helping to elicit the most characteristic pattern in which a motion event is encoded in Chinese. In this light, the two studies to be reviewed in this chapter provide the most representative model of motion in terms of event type.

Another feature of the two studies in this chapter is the group of languages involved: it exemplifies an ideal context in which each and every type of language in Talmy's motion event typology has been dealt with — the verb-framed Korean, the satellite-framed

English and the equipollently-framed Chinese. English and Korean stand at the two extremes of the satellite- and verb-framed continuum with opposing typological properties (e.g. path encoded in verb satellites in English whereas it is expressed in the main verb in Korean), yet the two are partially similar to (or different from) Chinese in their own way. Both Korean and English learners of Chinese confront with a challenging task of shifting from a linguistic system in which there is only one verb per clause to a new system with a multiple-part compound verb. This is not merely an issue of changing the lexicalisation pattern one is familiar with, but also a question of how to package multiple sematic components of motion into one compact grammatical category whilst presenting them as equally salient. What's more, both Korean and English have a single lexicalisation pattern for motion event encoding, whereas in Chinese, more than one structure exist to express motion events of varied types (e. g. *xiao 3 hai 2 ba 3 qiu 2 ti 1 guo 4 ma 3 lu 4* 'The boy kicked the ball across the street' and *xiao 3 hai 2 ti 1 zhe qiu 2 guo 4 ma 3 lu 4* 'The boy went across the street while kicking the ball'). In this sense, the L2 learners have to move from a relatively lucid pattern to a relatively ambiguous pattern, and the acquisition of the pattern atypical in their source language (e.g. the matrix-subordinated construction with *zhe* clause) may present a particularly hard task for them. In short, as a whole, the three languages with their distinctive typological properties constitute a complete and most intriguing triad for studies of motion event expressions.

Chapter 2 Narrating Motion Events in an L2—Evidence from English and Korean Learners of Chinese

2.1 How English learners across proficiencies acquire motion expressions in Chinese: A review of study by Ji (2021)

In this production task, the author investigates how English learners of Chinese at three proficiencies (i.e. low, intermediate and advanced) acquire typical motion expressions, the compound verb in particular.

Verb compounding is a quite frequently occurring phenomenon in Chinese (Li & Thompson, 1981). Multiple aspects of a given event can be conveniently packaged in a compound which is normally made up of two or three ingredients. Take the encoding of motion event as an example, the manner of motion, the path of motion and the deixis of motion can be simultaneously encoded in a compound verb such as *pao* 3 *guo* 4 *lai* 2 'run-cross-come'. The first constituent in the compound usually encodes a specific action such as manner of motion in motion event expressions; the second (sometimes along with the third) encodes the result of this action such as the concept of displacement (i.e. the path of motion) in motion expressions. More instances of such Chinese compounds include *da* 3 *sui* 4 'break-into pieces', *chi* 1 *wan* 2 'eat-finish', *gan* 3 *zou* 3 'drive-away from the speaker', etc.

For an L2 learner, the acquisition of resultative Chinese compound verb involves several aspects. In the first instance, the internal structure of Chinese verb compound is quite flexible and the compound can take various forms as needed. The second constituent in the compound verb, which is the path-encoding part in motion expressions, can stand on its own and function as an independent verb. This stands in stark contrast with the path-encoding verb particle in English, which does not possess any syntactic independence (e. g. *Mao* 1 *pa* 2 *shang* 4 *shu* 4 'The cat climbed up the tree'; please compare: *Mao* 1 *shang* 4 *le shu* 4 'The cat ascended the tree' vs. * The cat up the tree). In fact, every constituent in the compound verb can function independently, and any two of them can freely combine to present events with different semantic foci (e.g. *pao* 3 *guo* 4 'run across' [manner + path]; *pao* 3 *lai* 2 'run towards the speaker' [manner + deixis]; *guo* 4 *lai* 2 'cross towards the speaker' [path + deixis]).

Apart from the highly flexible internal structure, there is a fixed ordering sequence between constituents of the verb compound in Chinese. Again, let us take motion expressions as a case in point. The second constituent denoting path of motion forms a closed-class set in Chinese, which is standardly believed to have 7 members only, viz., *shang* 4 'ascend/up', *xia* 4 'descend/down', *jin* 4 'enter/into', *chu* 1 'exit/out of', *guo* 4 'cross/across', *hui* 2 'return/back' and *dao* 4 'arrive/to'. In a similar fashion, the deixis-denoting third constituent in a compound verb normally refers to either a direction towards the speaker (i.e. *lai* 2 'come/towards') or that away from the speaker (i.e. *qu* 4 'go/away from'). In comparison, the first constituent in a Chinese compound verb belongs to an open-class set with a considerably large number of members such as a variety of manner verbs in motion expressions (e.g. *run, jump, climb, jog, skate*, etc.). It is the combination of a large open-class set with a small closed-class set that results in the high productivity of Chinese compound verbs. In terms of ordering between constituents, the principle to abide by is as follows: the manner-encoding constituent always precedes path- and deixis-denoting constituents (e.g. *pa* 2 *shang* 4 *lai* 2 'climb up towards' vs. * *shang* 4 *lai* 2 *pa* 2 'up towards climb'), and the path-encoding ingredient should be put in front of the deixis-denoting component (e.g. *shang* 4 *lai* 2 'ascend

Chapter 2 Narrating Motion Events in an L2—Evidence from English and Korean Learners of Chinese

towards' vs. * *lai* 2 *shang* 4 'towards ascend'). Such an ordering sequence is in correspondence with the iconicity principle in cognition (Haiman, 1985). It reflects the temporal sequence between action and result in motion event encoding, that is, the manner of motion and the path of motion either coincide along the temporal axis (i.e. climbing whilst ascending) or immediately follow each other (climbing and ascending).

The third aspect to be acquired for an L2 learner is the grammatical status of a Chinese compound verb: is it a lexicon or a phrase? Chao (1968) suggests that the compound verb represents a process of morphological variation in which several verb roots are combined into a single verb root. It is also a single-stress phonological unit. This view is echoed with that of Li & Thompson (1981) who argue that the Chinese compound verb is a multiple-syllable unit with the property of a single verb despite that it can be decomposed into several meaningful morphemes. By this it is meant that in usage (particularly the usage of two-part compound verb), the perfective aspectual marker *le* in Chinese should be put at the end of the whole compound verb rather than at the end of the first manner-specifying constituent (please compare: *pa* 2 *shang* 4 *le shu* 4 'climb up *le* the tree' vs. * *pa* 2 *le shang* 4 *shu* 4 'climb *le* up the tree'). In a similar fashion, any noun phrase specifying the place as a frame of reference for motion needs to be affixed to the compound verb as a whole rather than to the first constituent in the compound (please compare: *pao* 3 *guo* 4 *ma* 3 *lu* 4 'run across the street' vs. * *pao* 3 *ma* 3 *lu* 4 *guo* 4 'run the street across').

To sum up, an L2 learner of Chinese needs to understand that verb compounding is highly frequent in Chinese and it plays a crucial role in the lexicalisation pattern of motion events in this language. Further, there is no finite vs. non-finite distinction between constituents in a compound verb. All components are equal in terms of syntactic function (i.e. each can be used as an independent verb and combine with others to form a new verb) and semantic function (i.e. each denotes a different aspect of a given event: manner, path or deixis). In this light, the study of Ji (2021) compares the performance of L2 learners in production tasks with that of Chinese monolinguals with respect to three questions:

a. Whether, and how, the L2 learners have acquired the internal structure of Chinese compound verbs including its constituents, the ordering principles of multiple constituents and the lexical status of compound verb as a whole.
b. Whether, and how, the L2 learners have acquired the systematic correspondence between semantic components and grammatical categories (i.e. the lexicalisation pattern of motion expressions in Chinese).
c. Whether, and how, the L2 learners have acquired the typical syntactic construction in which the compound verbs are used (i.e. in simplex clause).

The participants of the study Ji (2021) are recruited from overseas students in a university in Beijing, who come from three countries of the US, the UK and Australia. All L2 learners take English as their only native language, and Chinese as their only second language, which they have been learning for at least 6 months prior to the experiment. Their proficiency levels (i.e. advanced, intermediate and elementary) are determined according to their scores in the HSK tests held within 6 months before the start of the experiment.

The stimuli of this study comprise sixteen 5-second video clips

Chapter 2 Narrating Motion Events in an L2—Evidence from English and Korean Learners of Chinese

showing all kinds of spontaneous motion with a protagonist moving in a specific manner along a given path. Following the definition of Slobin (1996), manner of motion in these stimuli refers to the motor pattern in movement such as *jumping*, *running* and *walking*, the rate of movement such as *jogging* or *rushing*, the scheme of motion like *trudging* or *striding*, the attitude associated with the movement such as *ambling* or *strolling*, and the movement involving the use of instruments such as *skating*, *skiing* or *rowing*. The design of the study is as such that three kinds of manner are presented: a) general manner (e.g. *walking*, *running*, *jumping*), b) specific manner (e. g. *limping*, *jogging*, *skipping*), and c) manner with instruments (e.g. *walking on stilts*, *bicycling*, *sledging*). These manners are combined with four kinds of path: a) vertical path (*up*, *down*), b) boundary-crossing (*into*, *out of*), c) deixis (*towards*, *away from*) and d) path parallel to the reference point of motion (*along*, *around*).

During the administration of the experiment, the participants are requested to narrate what they have seen to an imagery listener. They have been asked a general question of ' What happened?' rather than any specific questions purposefully eliciting manner or path information (e.g. ' How did the boy walk?'). Most participants produce a single utterance to describe the motion scenes, which can be a simplex clause (e.g. *xiao 3 hai 2 zou 3 xia 4 lou 2 ti 1* ' The boy walked down the stairs'), a matrix-subordinate clause (e.g. *Xiao 3 hai 2 zou 3 zhe xia 4 le lou 2 ti 1* ' The boy went down the stairs while walking') or a sentence with juxtaposed or coordinated clauses (e. g. *Xiao 3 hai 2 zheng 4 zai 4 zou 3, ran 2 hou 4 xia 4 le lou 2 ti 1* ' The boy is walking, and then going down the stairs').

The target clause for each utterance is selected following two principles: a) the principle of semantic density: the clause encoding a higher number of motion components is the target for an analysis (e.g. 'He is walking into the bedroom [target]. He is walking very slowly'); b) the principle of first response: in cases where more than two clauses with the same semantic density are produced, the first naturally given response (rather than an elicited one) is chosen as the target (e.g. 'He is limping [target], and he went into the room').

The coding methodology of the study basically serves the three research questions to be dealt with. First of all, as regards the L2 acquisition of the formal structure of Chinese compound verbs, three verbal forms are distinguished: a) typical compound verbs: verbs including both manner- and path-denoting constituents, optionally along with deixis-denoting elements (e. g. *pao* 3 *guo* 4 *lai* 2 'run cross come', *pao* 3 *guo* 4 'run cross'); b) single verbs: single constituents specifying either manner or path of motion (e.g. *pao* 3, *guo* 4); c) atypical compound verbs: all forms of Chinese compound verbs expect for those in a) (e.g. *pao* 3 *lai* 2 'run come', *guo* 4 *lai* 2 'cross come'). With respect to the acquisition of lexicalisation pattern of motion events in Chinese, the study specifically investigates where across an utterance the semantic components of manner and path are encoded. Three loci are defined: a) in the first (or the second) constituent in a compound verb (e.g. *pao* 3 *guo* 4 'run cross'), b) in single verbs (e.g. *pao* 3, *guo* 4) and c) in other loci including adverbials, adverbs, prepositions, or even nouns (e.g. 'He is going as if he has broken his leg' [manner in adverbials], 'He is going from the top to the bottom' [path in prepositional phrases], 'skater', 'runner' [manner in nouns]). Finally, about the typical syntactic construction in which a compound verb occurs, three structures are explored: simplex clauses, complex clauses and coordinated clauses.

Responses elicited are analyzed both quantitatively and qualitatively, using appropriate statistical tools and methods. There are several major findings. Firstly, in terms of verbal forms used, both monolingual speakers of Chinese and L2 learners across proficiencies opt to use typical compound verbs most frequently, as compared to their uses of single verbs and atypical forms of compound verbs. However, their frequency of using typical Chinese compound verbs greatly varies: monolingual speakers and advanced learners of Chinese use compound verbs significantly more frequently than L2 learners of intermediate and low proficiencies. No differences are attested, however, between the former two groups, amongst whom no instances of atypical compound verbs are observed. A qualitative look at the data reveals that when L2 learners of relatively low proficiencies do use Chinese compound verbs, their usage is generally correct with only sporadic instances of over-generalisation in encoding paths parallel to ground of motion (e.g. * *tiao* 4 *wei* 2 'jump-around' vs. *wei* 2 *zhe* ... *tiao* 4 'jump surrounding'). When L2 learners use Chinese perfective aspectual marker *le* to signal the completion of an action, they, in most cases (97%), add this marker to the end of the compound verb as a whole rather than to the end of the first constituent.

Secondly, the author investigates the overall semantic density of elicited utterances and distinguishes three levels: utterances encoding simultaneously manner and path of motion (Manner + Path), and those encoding only one type of motion component (Manner-only and Path-only). The statistical analysis shows that in each participant group, utterances encoding both manner and path constitute the predominating majority as compared to the semantically less dense responses. Across groups, it is found that monolinguals and advanced learners of Chinese most frequently encode manner of motion in the first constituent of the compound verb, whereas learners of intermediate and low proficiencies more frequently use a single verb to express manner. In a similar fashion, monolinguals and advanced learners tend to encode path of motion in the second constituent of the compound verb, which stands in stark contrast with beginners who show a tendency of encoding path in an independent verb.

A qualitative examination of the data further reveals the following tendencies:

a. Advanced L2 learners tend to use most frequently typical forms of Chinese compound verbs and produce most frequently semantically dense utterances. In comparison, the frequency of using compound verbs is significantly lower in the group of beginners who seem to rely on independent verbs to encode single motion components from time to time.

b. Chinese monolinguals show a clear pattern of encoding a given semantic component using multiple grammatical devices, a tendency which has been discussed in some previous studies (e.g. Ji, 2014). For example, in the response *Ta* 1 *cong* 2 *wu* 1 *wai* 4 *man* 4 *man* 4 *de bo* 3 *xing* 2 *zhe zou* 3 *jin* 4 *wo* 4 *shi* 4 'He limped into the bedroom very slowly from the outside', the manner of motion is expressed, in the first instance, in the compound verb (i.e. *zou* 3 'walk'), then in the adverbial (i.e. *bo* 3 *xing* 2 *zhe* 'limping'), and further in the adverb describing the rate of walking (i.e. *man* 4 *man* 4 *de* 'slowly'). Similarly, the path of motion is twice encoded in the second constituent of the compound verb (i.e. *jin* 4 'enter/into') and in the prepositional phrase denoting the starting point of the motion (i.e. *cong* 2 *wu* 1 *wai* 4 'from the outside'). It is

Chapter 2 Narrating Motion Events in an L2—Evidence from English and Korean Learners of Chinese

worth noting that not a single response of 'multiple encoding', one of the defining features of elicited Chinese utterances, has been observed in L2 learners across groups, including those at the advanced level.

In relation to the above-discussed two findings, the study further suggests that all participant groups tend to use simplex clauses to encode motion events as compared to other syntactic constructions of complex sentences and coordinated clauses. Despite this, the frequency of using coordinated and juxtaposed clauses is significantly higher in learners of intermediate and low proficiencies than in advanced learners as well as monolingual speakers of Chinese. The former groups of participants more frequently encode manner and path in separated clauses, thus producing syntactically loose structures from time to time. It is worth mentioning that such a way of presenting manner and path in separation is not in line with the iconicity principle in cognition. Semantic components that have been presented as equally salient and occurring simultaneously should, in principle, be represented within the boundary of a single grammatical unit. Since participants in this study are all cognitively mature students, they should have been fully aware of this requirement. However, under the challenge of the communicative task of the experiment (i.e. to describe the events as fully as possible to an imagery audience) and the restriction of their language skills, the participants of low proficiencies seem to have sacrificed syntactic brevity to meet the communicative purpose of the task.

To sum up, the main findings of Ji (2021) reveal that in acquiring compound verbs, English learners of Chinese show evidences of generally learning the internal structure of the form, acknowledging the lexical status of the compound as a whole, and at the same time, largely getting rid of the 'verb polarity' feature in their source language and getting accustomed to the specific lexicalisation pattern in Chinese, viz., the simultaneous projection of multiple semantic components onto a compound form of grammatical category. As compared to monolingual speakers of Chinese, advanced L2 learners demonstrate target-like performance whereas learners of relatively low proficiencies do not seem to have fully acquired the target form. Specifically, they use Chinese compound verbs at a significantly low frequency and tend to utilize atypical grammatical categories such as single verbs rather than compound verbs to encode semantic components of motion events. In doing this, they have distributed multiple motion ingredients across utterances in a syntactically loose construction (e.g. coordination or juxtaposition), thus producing a less dense and less tight pattern of information packaging. It is to be noted that 'acquisition' seems to be better understood as an issue of degree. Although advanced L2 learners of Chinese have virtually acquired the compound verbs in motion expressions, their narration does not include even a single instance of multiple encoding of semantic components as demonstrated by monolingual speakers, which makes their utterances still less 'thick' in terms of semantic density. Meanwhile, despite that L2 learners of Chinese with low proficiencies hardly fully acquire the target verbal form, they seem to have a general mastery of the structure and the semantic requirements of the compound verb when they indeed use them.

Overall, the results of Ji (2021) suggest that the L2 acquisition is more like a dynamic process of changing one's thinking pattern associated with the source language and acquiring a new way of thinking compatible with the target language. In the particular study we review, the two languages share some typological features (i.e.

Chapter 2 Narrating Motion Events in an L2—Evidence from English and Korean Learners of Chinese

both have satellite-framed properties) rather than showing completely opposing features (e.g. the larger typological distance between English [and by extension Germanic languages] and Spanish [and by extension Romance languages]). Despite such partial typological similarity between English and Chinese, the acquisition of Chinese compound verbs still looks like a daunting task for L2 learners, particularly those of relatively low proficiencies, a phenomenon indicating that the acquisition of language skills is probably accompanied by a switch of grammatical concepts or a reintegration of new way of thinking into one's thought pattern fostered in the childhood in an L1 context.

2.2 How Korean learners across proficiencies acquire motion expressions in Chinese: A review of study by Jin (2020)

The study to be reviewed in the following investigates how speakers of a verb-framed language learn to encode motion events in Chinese. Since it utilizes the same set of stimuli and follows similar experimental procedures as elaborated in Section 2.1 above, it constitutes an interesting complementation to the study of Ji (2021) and provides a fresh insight into the nature of L2 acquisition of motion expressions.

The two languages under investigation are Chinese and Korean. As shown in previous discussion, Chinese is typically equipollently-framed with different semantic aspects of a motion event conveniently packaged into a compound verb, leading to utterances of syntactically tight construction and semantically dense cases. Korean, in contrast, belongs to verb-framed languages and thus parallels with most Romance languages such as Spanish and French.

The most distinctive feature of such languages is that the central semantic element for motion, which is path, is characteristically encoded in the main verb of an utterance, thus showing a lexicalisation pattern of conflating path of motion with the motion *per se* in the most important grammatical category of the main verb. This stands in sharp contrast with satellite-framed languages such as English in which manner of motion is encoded in the main verb and possesses a high degree of semantic salience.

Chinese and Korean are typologically partially similar in the sense that path is encoded in the main verb. The two, however, differ greatly at the same time, in their encoding of manner of motion. In satellite- and equipollently-framed languages such as English and Chinese, there is normally a large size and diversity of manner expressions such as many ways of walking (e. g. *hopping*, *jumping*, *leaping*, *limping* in English and *yu* 2 *yue* 4 ' leaping ', *bo* 3 *xing* 2 ' limping ', *da* 4 *ta* 4 *bu* 4 *zou* 3 ' striding ', *xiao* 3 *pao* 3 ' trotting ' in Chinese). Expressing manner of motion in these languages thus involves a relatively ' less heavy ' cognitive processing load in terms of production and comprehension. Every main clause has a finite verb and no additional syntactic effort is required to produce phrases such as ' limp into '. Verb-framed languages, in comparison, have to use lower-frequency non-finite forms such as adverbials and gerunds to express the same meaning (i.e. ' enter limping '; see Slobin [1996: 200-210] for a detailed discussion with a language pair of English and Spanish as a case in point). Due to the easy accessibility of lexical items to express manner, languages like English and Chinese are usually referred to as ' manner-salient ' languages. In contrast, in the verb-framed Korean, manner expressions can be readily omitted as long as it represents a default way of moving for a protagonist, for example, *walking* for a human being and *swimming* for a fish. It is

Chapter 2 Narrating Motion Events in an L2—Evidence from English and Korean Learners of Chinese

only in cases whereas the manner of motion is less default and needs to be verbally encoded that a separate grammatical device is recruited to do the job such as an adverbial, a gerund or a prepositional phrase (e.g. 'He rolls down' vs. 'He goes rolling down'; 'He crawls' vs. 'He goes on all fours').

As far as Korean is concerned, path is typically expressed in a bi-verbal construction which is made up of a path verb encoding the specific trajectory and an indispensable deictic verb expressing the direction of motion (note that this is different from the third constituent in a Chinese compound verb which only offers additional information about motion and is optional in nature). When there is a need to express manner of motion, Korean usually recruits a separate verb in a subordinated clause or a gerund. Given that Korean is a head-final language, a motion event is typically encoded as follows: *entek mith-ulo kwull-e nayly-e ka* 'It goes, rolling down the hill.' (qtd. in Jin 2020:7). In this example, path of motion is encoded in the main verb *nayly* 'descend', and deixis of motion is expressed in another verb *ka* 'go'. Since manner of motion is salient, it is expressed in a subordinated verb (i.e. *kwull-e* 'rolling') of the adverbial *entek mith-ulo kwull-e* 'rolling down the hill'). In this light, for Korean learners of Chinese, the most challenging task should be to learn to fully understand the salience of manner dimension in representing motion events in the L2 Chinese and to further acquire the language-specific way of manner encoding.

Participants of the study Jin (2020) are recruited from Korean students studying in a Chinese university where they have been systematically and intensely studying Chinese for at least two years. They have been classified as either advanced learners with HSK[①]

---

① HSK = Han4yu3 Shui3ping2 Kao3shi4 (Test of Chinses as a Second Language) ranking of 5 - 6 grades or low-intermediate learners with their HSK scores ranking from 2 - 4 grades (22 participants per group). Following similar strategies in experimental administration and in data transcribing and coding, Jin (2020) focuses on two issues: a) the acquisition of the structure of Chinese compound verbs, and b) the information density of elicited utterances including an overall semantic density of a response as well as local densities in given loci such as the main verb. The former issue investigates whether the L2 learners of Chinese have acquired the formal requirements of using a compound verb. The latter superficially explores how communicatively effective a response is; it investigates, in fact, whether the L2 learners have indeed acquired the lexicalisation pattern of motion expressions in Chinese, that is, conflating multiple semantic components into a compound verb (hence the particularly high information density at the locus of the main verb).

The main findings of this study can be summarized as follows (Jin, 2020: 28-32). First of all, in terms of the use of Chinese compound verbs, Jin (2020) classifies all verbal forms into three categories: a) typical compound verbs which are made up of a manner verb, a path verb and optionally a deictic verb, b) less typical verbs which mainly refer to the combinations of either manner verb + deictic verb or path verb + deictic verb, and c) single verb forms demonstrating manner of motion, path of motion, deixis of motion or simply general verbs denoting a general notion of displacement. The results of quantitative analyses suggest that the frequency of using typical compound verbs is significantly higher in the learner group of advanced participants than in the group of beginners, who use compound verbs at a significantly lower frequency as compared to their monolingual counterparts. In complementary to this, the percentage of single verbal forms is significantly higher amongst beginners than in the group of advanced learners. Further, learners across proficiencies use less typical compound verbs only occasionally. It is worth mentioning that such a tendency of using compound verbs amongst L2 learners is irrespective of path types, that is, the nature of the trajectory covered has virtually no influence on the use of specific verbal forms.

Secondly, as regards the issue of overall semantic density of utterances, and further, information density in specific loci, Jin (2020: 35-47) distinguishes, first of all, three types of utterance density (UD): responses encoding both manner (M) and path (P) of motion (M +P: UD =2), those encoding manner of motion only (M only: UD =1) or path of motion only (P only: UD =1). It is found that within both groups of L2 learners, the percentage of responses with UD =2 is significantly higher than that of utterances with UD =1. Across groups, however, the advanced L2 learners produce semantically dense utterances (UD =2) significantly more frequently than learners of low proficiency, who seem to distribute motion components across clauses in coordination, thus producing target responses with only manner or path information from time to time. Again, such findings are found consistent across path types. No matter which trajectory is encoded (e.g. vertical or boundary-crossing), the participants are fully aware of the need to express manner at the same time in order to make their narration as accurate and informative as possible, as requested by the experimenter.

The question of local information density (LD) reveals more interesting results. Jin (2020) distinguishes the locus of verb, which refers to the main verb of an utterance, from the locus of satellites, which mainly include verb particles, prepositional phrases, adverbials, subordinated clauses, nouns, etc. In the locus of main verb, utterances with LD =2 are significantly more frequently observed in advanced learners than in learners of low proficiency, suggesting that the large majority of L2 learners with high proficiency have acquired the target lexicalisation pattern of conflating manner and path into a compound verb.

As far as the local density of satellites is concerned, it is attested that utterances with LD =1 is significantly more frequently produced in the group of advanced learners as compared to both L2 beginners and monolingual speakers of Chinese, whose responses are characterized by a pattern of LD =0 at the locus of satellites. For Chinese monolinguals, given that the key semantic ingredients of motion have already been compactly packaged in a compound verb, there is no absolute need, in principle, to elaborate on these components outside the verbal domain. A closer look at the responses of LD =1 at the locus of satellites reveals that when L2 learners indeed encode semantic information outside the compound verb, they express manner and path at comparable frequencies (e.g. *Ta* 1 *yong* 4 *shuang* 1 *shou* 3 *shuang* 1 *jiao* 3 *dong* 4 'He is moving, using both hands and feet' [manner in adverbial]; *Ta* 1 *cong* 2 *shan* 1 *shang* 4 *fan* 1 *gun* 3 'He is rolling from the top of the hill' [path in prepositional phrase]). It needs to be noted that such a tendency as demonstrated by L2 learners is completely different, in nature, from the performance of monolingual speakers. When the latter group of speakers encodes additional information outside the compound verb and thus gives semantically particularly rich utterances, they choose to encode manner *per se* or path *per se* within the compound and additional information about manner and/or path in satellites. In this light, exemplified instances above will be typically encoded by Chinese monolinguals as follows: *Ta* 1 *yong* 4 *shuang* 1 *shou* 3 *shuang* 1 *jiao* 3 *pa* 2 *guo* 4 *qu* 4 'He is crawling past, using both hands and feet' [manner *per se* in compound verb; manner details in

Chapter 2 Narrating Motion Events in an L2—Evidence from English and Korean Learners of Chinese

adverbial]; *Ta* 1 *cong* 2 *shan* 1 *shang* 4 *gun* 3 *xia* 4 *lai* 2 ' He is rolling down towards the speaker from the top of the hill' [path *per se* in compound verb; source of path in prepositional phrase]). In other words, when monolinguals encode manner or path details in satellites, they use such additional semantic information to complement the motion components in the main verb, thus producing responses with particularly dense information. L2 learners, however, use semantic information in satellites to substitute motion components they should have otherwise encoded in the compound verb, a tendency that can be evidenced by their use of general verbs (e.g. *moving, going*), rather than specific manner and path verbs, in conjunction with manner or path satellites (e.g. *moving* [vs. *crawling*] in conjunction with *using both hands and feet*; *going* [vs. *descending*] in conjunction with *from the top of the hill*).

To sum up, the main findings of Jin (2020) indicate that for Korean learners of Chinese, the process of acquiring compound verbs seems to be challenging and it is particularly so for beginners. Though as adults, they are fully aware of the communicative purpose of the experiment and have produced responses with information density comparable to that of monolingual speakers of Chinese, their performance significantly differs from that of monolinguals in varied aspects such as the frequency of using typical compound verbs and local sematic density outside the verb domain.

Taking into account the results from the two studies reviewed above, it might be said that the acquisition of motion expressions in an additional language is a relatively hard process and closely related, among other things, to the proficiency level an L2 learner has reached. Note that the particular difficulty an L2 learner of low proficiency has encountered in their acquisition is set in a context in which their source language (i.e. English and Chinese, and Korean and Chinese, respectively) and the target language bear partial similarity in motion event typology. Despite such advantages, completely changing or switching one's language pattern cultivated from the childhood and fully acquiring the target language system still look like somewhat daunting. Overall, these results suggest that an L2 acquisition of motion language seems to be tied with a reintegration of conceptual systems and is well worth exploring at the cognitive level.

Chapter 3
Motion Event Cognition in Bilingual Speakers

Human beings' non-linguistic spatial understanding is believed to be universal because ' our ability to perceive and interpret spatial relationships is supported by vision and other highly structured biological systems such as the haptic-kinaesthetic system ' (Bowerman, 1999: 387). However, our linguistic systems exhibit striking variations in spatial description that do not reflect this perceptual and cognitive contour. This rich diversity in linguistic encoding of spatial events (motion in particular) has been widely documented in previous studies (Allen et al., 2007; Ji et al., 2011a, 2011b, 2011c; Beavers et al., 2010; Berman & Slobin, 1994; Choi & Bowerman, 1991; Filipovic & Jaszczolt, 2012; Slobin, 2004, to name a few). It has been suggested that this effect of language can penetrate to the cognitive level, affecting how speakers of different languages conceptualise motion events in nonlinguistic tasks (See, for instance, Athanasopoulos & Bylund, 2013; Ji & Hohenstein, 2017; Flecken et al., 2014; Gullberg, 2011; Hohenstein, 2005; Levinson, 2003; Slobin, 1996; Zlatev, 2011; Zlatev & Blomberg, 2015).

3.1 Representing motion events in an L2 context

The aforementioned observations have led to a revival of the linguistic relativity hypothesis in relation to space over the past three decades. However, the extension of the topic to the area of bilingualism is still a relatively new undertaking. The main arguments of the linguistic relativity hypothesis, also known as the 'Sapir-Whorf hypothesis' (Whorf, 1956), focus on how properties of a given language influence the structure and content of thought, thus affecting the way that humans view reality. As later illustrated by Slobin (1996), one's native language is not a neutral coding system of an objective reality; instead, it trains its speakers, from childhood, to pay habitual attention to specific dimensions of experience that are already enshrined in grammatical categories. Seen in this way, acquiring a native language entails learning a particular way of thinking ('Thinking for speaking' hypothesis in Slobin, 1996: 76-89). Such an effect of linguistic relativity has been reported in some investigations conducted across different groups of language speakers, and in varied domains, such as colour perception, object categorisation, temporal representation, space and motion events (see, for instance, Boroditsky, 2001; Hohenstein, 2005; Levinson, 2003; Lupyan, 2012; Regier & Kay, 2009; Zlatev & Blomberg, 2015). Given that a particular language instantiates a special way of thinking, and that differences in linguistic structure foster variations in cognitive pattern, one naturally wonders what would happen to people who have two or more languages at their disposal. Do they look at the world differently from monolingual speakers? The linguistic relativity hypothesis can thus have far-reaching consequences for a number of important issues in L2 acquisition, which include the following questions: To what extent does an L2 learner recalibrate his cognitive dispositions as a result of additional language learning? What is the nature of the relationship between progress in L2 acquisition and the shifting cognitive state of an L2 speaker? What are the (extra) linguistic factors that determine the language-specific cognitive behaviour of an L2 speaker in nonverbal tasks (Ji, 2018: 26; as discussed in Bylund & Athanasopoulos, 2014: 953-954).

3.2 Manner-salience in English and Manner- and Path-salience in Chinese

In addition to Motion itself, Talmy (1985, 2000) conceptualises motion events as consisting of Figure, Ground, Path and Manner. He further proposes a dichotomy between satellite-framed and verb-framed languages in motion description. English has been widely accepted as a representative satellite-framed language. In such languages, the main verb describes the Manner or form of motion (e.g. *climbing*), while the Path or destination of motion is encoded by a 'satellite' (e.g. a verb particle like *up*). Research has shown that the satellite-framedness of English is highly systematic across different types of motion events (e.g. spontaneous and caused motion) and different learner types (e.g. children and adults), under various experimental situations (e.g. naturalistic and elicitation tasks) and in different genres of discourse (e.g. oral production and literary discourse).

In stark contrast to the clear-cut typological picture of English, the situation in Mandarin Chinese is much more complicated. A motion event is typically expressed in Chinese through a verb compound, which usually consists of three components: C1 (Manner verb) + C2 (Path element) + C3 (optional; Deictic element; e.g. *pa* 2 *shang* 4 *qu* 4 ' climb-ascend/up-go/thither ')[①]. There are

---

[①] C (as in C1, C2, C3) stands for 'component'.

different views on the grammatical category of C2 and C3, though C1 is agreed to be a verb. On the one hand, C2 and C3 are like English particles: both belong to a closed-class set and are limited in number. Seen from this perspective, Chinese can be taken as satellite-framed (Talmy, 1985, 2000). On the other hand, components like C2 and C3 differ syntactically from English particles since they can function as independent verbs (e.g. *Hou 2 zi shang* 4 *le shu* 4 'The monkey ascended the tree'). In this sense, Slobin (2004) argues that most serial verb languages, like Chinese and Thai, should stand on their own and form a third group of 'equipollently-framed languages' (see also Ji *et al.*, 2011a; Chen, 2005; Chu, 2009; Gao, 2001; Chen & Guo, 2009; Zlatev & Yangklang, 2004).

In experimental studies concerning description of spontaneous motion events, researchers have found that Chinese departs from English in many aspects. In Slobin's (2004) investigation of the '*Frog, Where Are You?*' oral narratives, he observed that Chinese adults and children across ages used Manner verbs and Path verbs to describe given scenes roughly equally frequently (i.e. example 4a and example 4b).

3. English:
The owl flew out of a hole in a tree.

4. Chinese:
   a. *Mao* 1 *tou* 2 *ying* 1   *fei* 1-*chu* 1 *le*   *shu* 4 *dong* 4.
      owl   fly-out of ASP   tree   hole
    'The owl flew out of a hole in a tree.'
   b. *Mao* 1 *tou* 2 *ying* 1 *pai* 1 *da* 3 *zhe* *chi* 4 *bang* 3 *cong* 2 *dong* 4
      owl   flap   DUR wing   from hole
     li 3   *chu* 1 *lai* 2 *le*.

inside　　exit-come　　ASP
'The owl, flapping its wings, exited a hole in a tree.' ①

Similarly, Ji *et al.* (2011c) systematically investigate the ways that Chinese adults and children describe spontaneous motion events illustrating specific Manner (e.g. *walking*, *cycling*, *crawling*) and Path information (e.g. *up*, *down*, *into*, *across*). Their results reveal that, even though we take C2 and C3 in Chinese verb compounds as 'satellites' and thus temporarily classify Chinese and English as both satellite-framed, about 25 per cent of spontaneous motion events in Chinese are expressed in quite different ways from English. This is particularly evident in examples using a tool or vehicle (e.g. bicycle; please compare examples 5a and 5b).

5. a. A woman cycled across the railway tracks.
　b. *Ta* 1　　*qi* 2　　*zhe*　　*zi* 4 *xing* 2 *che* 1 *guo* 4　　*ma* 3 *lu* 4.
　　 She　　ride　　DUR　　bicycle　　　　　　cross　　street
　'She, riding her bicycle, went across the railway tracks.'

In examples 4b and 5b above, Chinese demonstrates some clear typological features of a verb-framed language in that the main verb of the sentence conflates Path of motion (i.e. *guo* 4 'cross'; and *chu* 1 *lai* 2 'exit-come', respectively). However, Manner of motion is encoded in satellite-type elements (i.e. *pai* 1 *da* 3 *zhe chi* 4 *bang* 3 'flapping its wings' and *qi* 2 *zhe zi* 4 *xing* 2 *che* 1 'riding her bicycle', respectively).

Such a property of verb-framedness is even more pronounced in

---

① Abbreviations used in example 2 are as follows: ASP = aspectual perfective marker *le* in Chinese; DUR = durative aspectual marker *zhe* in Chinese.

the encoding of caused motion events. Ji *et al.* (2011b) conduct a systematic investigation of how Chinese children and adults linguistically describe a particular type of caused motion events as illustrated in the current study. It is reported that up to 70% of Chinese utterances recruit compound verbs in depicting complex motion events, and these compound forms invariably encode Manner, Path and (optionally) Deixis of motion (e.g. *tui* 1-*guo* 4 'push-cross'). The remaining 30% of responses express Path alone in a single verb (*guo* 4 'cross' as in 6c) whilst expressing Manner (and Causality) in a gerund, thus giving rise to a syntactic construction typical of verb-framed languages like French (i.e. the syntactic similarity between examples 6a and 6c).

6. a. Popi *traverse* la rue *en faisant rouler* le ballon.
'Bonny went across the street while pushing the ball.'
b. Bonny *ba* 3   *qiu* 2   *tui* 1 *guo* 4   *ma* 3 *lu* 4.
Bonny   *ba*   ball   push-across/cross   street
'Bonny pushed the ball across the street.'
c. Bonny *tui* 1   *zhe*   *qiu* 2   *guo* 4   *ma* 3 *lu* 4.
Bonny   push   gerund   ball   cross   street
'Bonny, pushing the ball, went across the street.'

Seen in this way, the exact typological status of Chinese in motion description remains a disputed issue, but researchers agree that Chinese is not typical of either satellite- or verb-framed languages; rather, it possesses characteristics of both types. Thus, it is better to view Chinese in an intermediate category that sits between satellite- and verb-framed groups or as standing midway along a satellite- vs. verb-framed continuum (see, for instance, Ji *et al.*, 2011a; Beavers *et al.*, 2010; Chen & Guo, 2009; Chu, 2009; Li,

1990; Slobin, 2004). In English, the marked grammatical category of verb encodes Manner of motion (i.e. Manner salience), whereas in Chinese, the same verbal domain packages Manner and Path simultaneously (equal salience of Manner and Path). Such language differences may have some cognitive implications. According to the linguistic relativity hypothesis, these language-specific properties affect a speaker's 'habitual behaviour', i. e., what speakers do most naturally, by default, in common situations. Although both Manner and Path are commonly encoded for motion expression in English and Chinese, the specific lexicalisation patterns of motion events in the two languages prompt their speakers to pay differing amounts of attention to the varied semantic dimensions of motion. English speakers are systematically shown how to place Manner information in arguably the most important grammatical category of an utterance, i. e., the verb. Indeed, they habitually attend to Manner in verbs in their representation of motion events. In contrast, Chinese speakers systematically meet Manner coupled with Path in the verb and they habitually conceptualise these two types of information as being equally salient and as occurring simultaneously.

Psychological frameworks, such as associative learning, can explain these effects of linguistic relativity. According to this theory, "representations build up, or emerge, over exposure to a number of specific instances of associations" (Athanasopoulos et al., 2015a: 141). Repeated exposures thus become part of an individual's cognitive routine and can lead to regularities in conceptualisation or behaviour. Seen in this way, Chinese speakers are repeatedly exposed to Manner and Path occurring together in a verb while English speakers are more familiar with Manner information occurring alone. "The more routinized an association becomes, the easier it is to retrieve and utilize it for purposes of categorisation" (Langacker, 2008; see Athanasopoulos *et al.*, 2015a: 141 for a detailed discussion). Thus, in a triads matching task, it is likely that English speakers more frequently utilise 'Manner-salience' as a basis for their nonverbal similarity judgments (i.e. more Manner-matches) whereas their Chinese counterparts recruit 'Manner-salience' and 'Path-salience' equally frequently as bases for their decision-making (e.g. comparable proportions of Manner- and Path-matches). In an L2 context, this mainly concerns the extent to which categorisation is influenced by a conceptual switch from the pattern of 'Manner-Path salience' to 'Manner salience'.

3.3 Motion event cognition in L2 learners

The striking cross-linguistic differences in terms of motion event typology prompts the question of whether motion cognition differs in speakers of languages with opposing properties. Research in this area produces contradictory results with some studies showing almost no obvious effect of language on thought (e.g. Gennari *et al.*, 2002; Jackendoff, 1996; Landau & Lakusta, 2006; Lucy, 1992; Papafragou *et al.*, 2002), while others suggest a clear effect of linguistic relativity (e.g. Boroditsky, 2001; Hohenstein, 2005; Levinson, 2003; Lupyan, 2012; Naigles & Terrazas, 1998; Zlatev & Blomberg, 2015), as examined in varied non-linguistic behavioural tasks, such as memory recognition, categorisation of motion events and preferential looking. When the linguistic relativity hypothesis is tested in the context of bilingual representation, the key issue is whether bilinguals' conceptualisation differs from that of monolinguals and, if so, how. Findings along this line, as attested in motion event cognition, seem to suggest that learning an additional language can result in conceptual restructuring or shifts in one's cognitive state (Athanasopoulos, 2009; Athanasopoulos *et al.*, 2015b; Brown & Gullberg, 2010; Bylund & Athanasopoulos, 2014; Cook & Bassetti, 2011; Daller *et al.*, 2011; Filipovic, 2011; Flecken *et al.*, 2015; Montero-Melis *et al.*, 2016; Pavlenko, 2011; Thierry, 2016).

To give an example, a growing number of studies examine the relationship between grammatical aspect (e.g. perfect vs. imperfect) and the representation of motion events. Many studies have revealed that the presence or absence of grammatical aspect in a language influences the degree that speakers pay habitual attention to the endpoints of motion (see, for instance, Athanasopoulos & Bylund, 2013; Bylund *et al.*, 2013; Flecken *et al.*, 2015; von Stutterheim *et al.*, 2012). To illustrate, in one type of language (e.g. German or Swedish), the verb does not have aspectual inflections and the speakers of these non-aspect languages tend to focus on the endpoint of a motion event, thus developing a holistic perspective of event (e.g. *She is walking towards the church*). In contrast, verbs in some other languages are marked for aspect (e.g. the progressive in English) and users of these aspect languages are inclined to direct their attention to the 'ongoingness' of an event, thereby taking an 'inside' view of a situation (e.g. *She is walking along the road [to the church]*; see Flecken *et al.*, 2015: 42-43 for a summary). This correlation between grammatical aspect and event endpoints is attested in behavioural tasks, such as eye movements in viewing motion screens, and motion event categorisation.

Extending this effect of language difference on visual perception of motion to the bilingual domain, the key question arises as to whether, and how, L2 learners can recalibrate their conceptual (or cognitive) propensity associated with L1 as a result of their additional language learning. Athanasopoulos *et al.* (2015b) address this question in a triads matching task by examining how English (aspect language focusing on 'ongoingness' of an event) learners of German (non-aspect language highlighting endpoints of motion event) match a target scene with an intermediate degree of endpoint tendency to two alternates showing high and low degrees of endpoint saliency. The purpose of the study is to find out whether L2 learners whose native language marks grammatical aspects can learn to start paying more attention to event endpoints in the course of acquiring a target, non-aspect language. It is reported that, compared to native speakers of English, learners of L2 German are more prone to base their similarity judgments on endpoint saliency, rather than ongoingness, primarily as a function of increasing proficiency and length of exposure. These results suggest that English learners of German may have internalised additional perspectives on event construal (i.e. endpoints apart from ongoingness), restructured the frames they have acquired in L1 and shifted their patterns of motion event representation. It is during this process that they have developed a cognitive state that increasingly biases towards the target language.

Athanasopoulos *et al*. 's (2015b) investigation represents studies focusing on how bilinguals shift towards L2 categorisation patterns as a function of L2 exposure in a relatively long period. Such studies are characterised by comparing behavioural performance between bilingual vs. monolingual groups. Another line of research in bilingual motion event cognition is to assess whether, and how, linguistic cues present in the immediate environment can be recruited by L2 learners to assist them in event categorisation or discrimination. Studies of this type normally concern only bilinguals, who perform behavioural tasks under manipulated linguistic conditions. As a case in point, Montero-Melis *et al.* (2016) investigate whether L2 priming affects similarity judgments in representing a complex type of caused motion (similar to stimuli in the present study). Specifically, Swedish (a satellite-framed language highlighting Manner information) adult learners of L2 Spanish (a verb-framed language highlighting Path information) are asked to read out loud L2 sentences with varying degrees of Manner or Path salience before arranging motion scenes. Results show that Path vs. Manner priming affects how participants judge the similarity between events. For example, immediately after reading out L2 sentences highlighting the Path dimension, Swedish adult learners tend to arrange motion events on a 'same-Path' basis. Note that this judging criterion is inconsistent with the typological feature of their native language, thus indicating that when linguistically mediated, cognitive restructuring can be dynamic and context-dependent, and a switch of conceptual representations in bilinguals can be completed in a relatively short time scale.

These findings echo those obtained by Lai & Narasimhan (2008) who examine how bilingual speakers of English and Spanish conceptualise motion events in a forced similarity judgment task. It is reported that bilinguals who describe a motion event in English in the first instance tend to select the event that has the same Manner of motion as the target scene significantly more frequently than bilinguals who encode the same event in Spanish prior to judgment. In a similar fashion, Filipovic (2011) tests whether balanced English-Spanish bilingual speakers behave like monolinguals in each of their languages when describing and remembering motion events with different types of Manner information. She finds that, regardless of the language used in the experiment, the performance of bilingual participants in the recognition task closely resembles that of the Spanish monolingual speakers. She attributes this to the status of Spanish as a 'dominant' language in the life of her bilingual participants.

Most studies of L2 motion cognition involve languages with opposing typological properties (e.g. satellite- vs. verb-framed). Very few studies have systematically explored the 'degree of difference' amongst languages in the same (or similar) typological category and the effect of such subtle linguistic differences on motion event cognition. One exception is the work of Czechowska and Ewert (2011), who argue that the group of satellite-framed languages are not homogeneous. For example, both English and Polish characteristically encode Manner in motion description, but the Path dimension has a higher degree of 'codability' in English than in Polish. They design similarity judgment and rating tasks to explore whether such minimal differences in motion lexicalisation pattern have cognitive implications. Their results show that English monolinguals pay more attention to Path in the rating task than their Polish counterparts when their attention is directed to more than one attribute of motion at the same time. Furthermore, Polish-English bilinguals behave like monolingual speakers of English in their attention to Path. There is a linear relationship between L2 proficiency and perception of motion events, clearly suggesting a shift towards L2 values. Such findings lead to Czechowska and Ewert's (2011) conclusion that a conceptual shift towards the L2 has already taken place in the least-proficient bilinguals and that reconstructing of the conceptual domain is evidenced in the two most proficient groups (2011: 308).

To summarise, studies of bilingual motion event cognition are in great need of expansion. Previous literature tends to focus on languages with contrasting typological features only (i.e. satellite- vs. verb-framed) and examine, in most cases, spontaneous motion events only (but see Montero-Melis *et al.* [2016] for an exception). In this context, the present study expands the pair of languages under investigation to include the non-Indo-European language of Chinese, which is typologically partially similar to English (rather than entirely in opposition to it). This will allow us to test whether the typological similarity between L1 and L2 (i.e. ' manner-salience ' in both languages) can facilitate L2 learners' cognitive restructuring in implicit processing. Specifically, it will investigate how Chinese adult L2 learners of English at different proficiencies conceptualise voluntary and caused motion events (i.e. motion involving path, causality and varied types of manner information) in a triads matching task. Their performance is then compared to that of Chinese and English monolingual speakers with the aim of shedding fresh light on the question of linguistic relativity recast in an L2 context: the extent to which nonverbal similarity judgments in relation to motion events in L2 learners are driven by the learner's native language (i.e. Chinese), or whether they show signs of restructuring in terms of the target language (i.e. English).

Chapter 4
The Conceptualisation of Voluntary Motion Events in L2 English Learners (Experiment 1)

The two experiments to be reported in Chapter 4 and Chapter 5 focus on second language (L2) motion event cognition in Chinese-English bilinguals (as compared to monolingual speakers) in a non-verbal similarity judgment task with the aim of revealing: a) the extent to which the L2 English learners can change the thought pattern associated with their first language (L1) and adjust their cognitive propensity in the direction of an L2, and b) the dynamic relationship between increasing proficiencies and stages of conceptual reconstructing in an L2 learner.

4.1 Predictions

Due to language-specific properties, we hypothesize, first of all, that Chinese monolinguals will be Manner- and Path-oriented in the behavioural task whereas their English counterparts will be predominately Manner-oriented. We speculate that the L2 Chinese learners of English at the initial stage of their acquisition will resemble Chinese monolinguals more closely and remain largely Manner- and Path-oriented. Only when L2 learners progress to

Chapter 4   The Conceptualisation of Voluntary Motion Events in L2 English Learners (Experiment 1)

higher levels of learning (e.g. at intermediate and advanced levels) will their behaviour become target-language-like and become largely Manner-oriented. This prediction is made after taking into account two arguments:

a. According to Slobin's (1996: 89) 'thinking for speaking' hypothesis, learning a second language means acquiring an alternative way of thinking. Therefore, the L1 'thinking for speaking' pattern, which is ingrained from one's childhood, should be resistant to reconstruction in adult second language learning. We speculate that this is particularly true at an early stage of acquisition.

b. Previous studies suggest that learning a second language involves changing one's existing concepts or developing new concepts (see, for instance, Pavlenko, 2011). We argue that this process needs to be completed and internalised over a longer period of time. Developmental changes in behaviour (if any) thus only occur at a later stage of acquisition.

Specifically, we predict two possibilities regarding the explicit measure of selection strategies and the implicit measure of processing time:

a. A strong version of the linguistic relativity hypothesis: A subtle effect of language on cognition is manifested in both overt choices and response latencies. Chinese monolinguals, as well as low proficiency L2 learners, will choose the Path-matched videos as most similar to the target video more often than English native speakers and relatively advanced L2 learners. Meanwhile, they will show more rapid processing of the Path dimension, as evidenced by their significantly shorter reaction time (RT) in judging videos with Path-similarity, presumably due to the higher linguistic codability of Path in the Chinese language.

b. A weak version of the linguistic relativity hypothesis: Variations in the thought pattern as produced by linguistic differences will only be attested at the automatic and implicit level of processing (i.e. the RT), but not at the explicit level of forced judgments (i.e. A or B choices). Following this argument, we expect Chinese monolinguals and low proficiency L2 learners of English to react significantly more quickly in judging Path-matched (rather than Manner-matched) videos, compared with English monolinguals and advanced L2 learners.

In terms of preferences in judgment, however, we predict that participants across groups will mainly choose Path-matched scenes. This prediction is based on the following observations:

a. The two languages under investigation in the present study do not have opposing typological properties in motion description (English and Chinese are partially similar), and this lesser magnitude of linguistic difference may not be strong enough to elicit different cognitive modes in behavioural tasks. ①

b. Path of motion (rather than Manner of motion) has cognitive salience in the conceptualisation of motion events (Talmy, 1985; Ibarretxe-Antunano, 2009). It is the most essential motion component, without which a motion event hardly exists. Note that prediction b is also supported by findings from some previous studies, which suggest that there is usually a divergence between explicit measure (e.g. decision strategies in the present study) and implicit measure (i.e. RT) of second language learning (see, for instance, Li *et al.*, 1993; Tokowicz & MacWhinney, 2005).

4.2 Methodology

4.2.1 *Participants*

One hundred and sixty adult students participated in the study; all were university or senior high school students. They were divided into five groups with thirty-two gender-balanced students per group.

---

① Some researchers suggest that the effect of language typology cannot go beyond language performance and influence cognition, even in the case of a language pair with dramatically different typological statuses (e.g. English vs. Spanish). This is because quite a number of languages show 'mixed' typological features and the linguistic differences in motion description can be considered, in some sense, as probabilistic (rather than categorical). Therefore, they are unlikely to produce differences in the thought pattern (e.g. Lupyan, 2012).

Chinese monolingual speakers came from a technical school of the Shandong Province in China and English native speakers (NS) were recruited from King's College, London. The three groups of adult Chinese learners of L2 English consisted of students from Shenzhen University, China. Permission to recruit and advertise the study was granted by the schoolmaster of the technical school in Shandong China, the Committee of Research Ethics of King's College, London and the Committee of Academic Affairs of Shenzhen University, respectively. Informed consent forms and demographic information sheets were collected from participants prior to the start of the experiment. All students received a monetary reward for their participation.

The proficiency levels of L2 learners (low, intermediate and advanced) were determined by their test scores in the English Language Proficiency Tests, administered twice a year by the Ministry of Education, China. This formal measure of general proficiency in the English language distinguishes three levels: Band 4 and Band 6 (for non-English major students) and Band 8 (for English major students). There are separate test papers for the three bands, with identical test paper design and scoring system, but different proficiency requirements in various aspects, such as listening, reading, writing, understanding and Chinese-English translating. All L2 learners in our study had taken the aforementioned tests in the six months before the experiment. The low proficiency level learners are students who had only passed the Band 4 test; the intermediate level students had passed the Band 6 test; those who had passed the Band 8 proficiency test were categorised as advanced learners and read L2 English as part of their degree in English language or literature. All L2 students (Mean age = 22.3 years) had taken these English proficiency tests 6 months or so prior to the experiment. They had

Chapter 4   The Conceptualisation of Voluntary Motion Events in L2 English Learners (Experiment 1)

similar learning backgrounds with systematic English input from around the age of twelve. They all acquired English in a predominately Chinese-speaking community and their English input mainly came from classroom teaching (See Table 1, below).

Table 1   Groups of participants in the study

Group ID	Age (M and SD)①	Proficiency level	Proficiency score (M and SD)	Length of L2 exposure	No. of participants
CHNS	19.30 (0.97)②	Chinese NSs	N/A	N/A	32
L2-Low	20.28 (1.76)	Elementary learners of English	70.97 (6.32)	7.19 years	32
L2-Medium	21.16 (1.14)	Intermediate learners of English	69.23 (6.23)	8.06 years	32
L2-High	24.77 (2.06)	Advanced learners of English	70.89 (6.70)	11.61 years	32
ENNS	26.00 (5.17)	English NSs	N/A	N/A	32

Note: L2-Low: second language learners of English (low proficiency); L2-Medium: second language learners of English (intermediate proficiency); L2-High: second language learners of English (advanced proficiency); CHNS: monolingual

---

① M = mean; SD = standard deviation.

② The group of monolingual speakers of Chinese does not match exactly with other groups in age and educational background (i.e. they are technical school students with a mean age of 19.30). This is because it is virtually impossible to recruit entirely and completely monolingual Chinese native speakers who are also educated to university level. We have made sure that the senior technical school students we recruited have only basic to lower knowledge of English due to the course design in their school.

Chinese native speakers, and ENNS: monolingual English native speakers.

4.2.2 Materials

The experimental stimuli consisted of 16 triads of video clips (5 seconds each) demonstrating spontaneous motion events. They all depicted a boy named Bonny performing a specific action (e.g. walking, running, hopping) along certain route (e.g. vertical: *up*, *down* ; boundary-crossing: *into*, *across* ; deixis: *towards*, *away from* and course parallel to the Ground of motion: *along*, *around*). In each triad, there were three video clips: a target and two alternates. Apart from the motion itself, these videos were identical in aspects such as the background scenery for motion and the protagonist's clothing in order to direct the participants' attention to actions rather than anything else and to help them understand that the judgments need to be made on the basis of similarities in actions.

In each triad, the video clips were played in a synchronised sequence. The target video was played first, in the central position of a black screen, for 5 seconds. After 0.5 seconds of a totally black screen, the two alternate videos appeared side-by-side on the same screen for 5 seconds. There was a 1 second black screen between triads. Compared with the target video clip, which incorporated both a Manner and a Path (e.g. Bonny hopped out of the bedroom), the Manner-matched alternate changed the trajectory of motion whilst keeping the Manner of motion intact (e.g. Bonny hopped *into* the bedroom) while the Path-matched alternate retained the Path of motion but altered the Manner of motion (e.g. Bonny *limped* into the bedroom). Appendix A shows a complete list of the 48 target and alternate actions, accompanied by an illustration the video stimuli used.

4.2.3 Pretest

A pretest for perseveration was administered prior to the testing session. Participants were shown five triads of static pictures showing ordinary objects, such as pigeons, flowers and bananas. Within each triad, the target object was placed in the centre of a piece of paper, while two alternates were shown side-by-side on a separate page, each differing from the target by either size only (e.g. a bunch of *big* bananas vs. a bunch of *small* bananas) or colour only (a bunch of *yellow* bananas vs. a bunch of *green* bananas). The participants were asked to identify which of the two alternates was most like the target object. If participants had chosen alternates from only one side of the page for all five selections (none did), they would have been considered perseverative and thus excluded from the study.

The term 'perseveration' here can be roughly understood as some form of response repetition or the inability to undertake set shifting (e.g. changing of behaviour, activities, etc.; see Helm-Estabrooks, 2004 for a detailed explanation). In our particular experimental set-up, a 'perseverative' participant would tend to choose the target motion scene from only one side of the screen. Since Manner- and Path-matched video clips alternate at the left (or right) position of the screen, this would systematically lead to an equal number of selections for Manner- and Path-matched scenes, thus failing to show any particular preference for either the Manner or the Path dimension. Therefore, we followed Hohenstein (2005) in the experimental procedures by excluding potential 'perseverative' participants from the study.

4.2.4 Testing session

The experiments were conducted in different locations in London and in China. Each location consisted of a quiet classroom (or seminar room) with no (or little) distraction for participants. Informed consent forms and demographic information sheets (e. g., age, course of study, parental education, language exposure) were gleaned from participants before the experiment.

The participants took part in the test individually. They were invited to view video clips played on a MacBook Pro and requested to judge the similarity between motion scenes by pressing one of the two keys on the keyboard: 'A' or 'L', respectively. These two keys were kept apart from each other on the keyboard and covered with white stickers (i.e. no linguistic labelling). If the participant felt that the alternate on the left side of the screen was most like the target, she should press down 'A'; otherwise, she chose the 'L' key.

There was a training triad prior to the test session (target: *The boy pulling a boat out of lake*), which aimed to familiarise the participants with test procedures and requirements. Participants were encouraged to make their decisions as quickly as possible. As soon as the training phase ended and the testing session started, the female experimenter removed herself from the participant's view by retreating to a far corner of the room. All video stimuli were played to the participants on the laptop screen through the stimulus presentation software 'SuperLab 4.5'. At the end of each session, a file was automatically generated by the software, which contained, among other things, participants' choices ('A' or 'L' key pressed) and the time they spent in making that choice (in ms).

Chapter 4　The Conceptualisation of Voluntary Motion Events in L2 English Learners (Experiment 1)

The stimuli were played in two randomised orders: A and B, which were counterbalanced across participants in a given group. The presentation position of Manner- or Path-matched videos (left or right side of the screen) was also counterbalanced in a given order. The stimuli were played in a synchronised series with the target videos playing first in the centre of a screen, followed by two simultaneous alternate videos placed side-by-side on the same screen. There was a black screen of 0.5 sec between a target and two alternates within each triad, and a 1 sec black screen between triads. The participant was instructed to view the stimuli and make his or her decisions as quickly as possible. Audio stimuli accompanying the video were: 'Target: This is X'. Alternates: 'Which one is most like X?'[①] In order to render the current study a truly 'non-linguistic' one, a verbal interference task was utilised in which a random sequence of numbers were broadcast to the participants throughout the testing phase, with the aim of preventing them from

---

[①] In the present study, the language of instruction (i.e. in the audio stimuli) for the learner groups is English, whereas the language context (on informed consent forms and demographic information sheets) is Chinese. Some recent studies suggest that the language involved in a nonverbal task may exert a context-bound and transient effect on bilingual cognition (but see Filipovic, 2011 for different findings). For instance, Athanasopoulos et al. (2015a) report that fluent German-English bilinguals categorise motion events according to the grammatical constraints of the language in which they operate. Other researchers have different observations suggesting that if bilingual groups have access to both languages during the task, any effects induced by language context may be effectively wiped out (see Montero-Melis et al., 2016: 640-642 for a detailed discussion).

subconsciously verbalising motion scenes during the process of their decision-making (see similar 'number-shadowing' tasks in Gennari *et al.*, 2002). The participants heard the same list of random numbers throughout the testing session and they were not required to repeat the numbers aloud.

4.2.5 Coding

Two sets of variables were adopted in data coding. The first type of measurement is categorical in nature and refers to participants' overt choices in decision making, as indicated by their pressing down of given keys ('A' or 'L') on the keyboard (i.e. either Manner-match or Path-match). This categorical variable aims to reveal whether there are differences across groups in terms of preference.

The other type of variable is continuous in nature and aims to test the degree of differences (if any) between groups. It refers to participants' latencies in response to different nonlinguistic stimuli, i. e., reaction time (RT). According to some previous studies (e.g. Hunt & Agnoli, 1991; Hunt & Banaji, 1988), differences in nonlinguistic cognition engendered by language differences will be more obvious in implicit processing or in speed of processing than in 'A or B' responses to classification tasks. This is because the processing variable enables us to judge the degree of difference rather than its presence or absence. Although few crosslinguistic studies have utilised RT measurements in behavioural tasks, Hunt and Banaji (1988) found that speakers of different languages spent subtly different amounts of processing time in judging the same situation, presumably due to their different ways of linguistically encoding the situation. In this light, the data coding in the present study combines overt preferences with implicit processing, with the aim of more precisely revealing any potential differences in nonlinguistic thought patterns produced by linguistic differences.

In our study, the participants were given an instruction sheet immediately prior to the experiment. The instructions clearly requested that participants 'make their choices as quickly as possible'. The RT for a given stimulus was calculated from the onset of alternate videos to the completion of a given triad, including a 1 second black screen immediately following the end of alternate videos. Theoretically, the longest RT could be 6000 ms. However, the participants were told that they did not have to wait until they had seen alternate videos in their entirety. By excluding extremely short values (button pressed within 200 ms of stimulus onset), 93 out of 2559 values were removed from the RT data. A prior screening for outliers was conducted by removing all observations that were at a distance of more than two standard deviations (SD) from the group mean for long RTs, and 204 observations out of a total of 2559 were cleaned.

4.3 Results

Using both categorical choices and continuous measurements, this section investigates: a) whether, and how, monolingual speakers' decision strategies differ significantly from those of L2 learners; b) whether, and how, typological variations in motion description lead to behavioural differences between Chinese and English monolingual speakers; and c) whether, and how, the behaviour of L2 learners differs as a result of their progression in language proficiency.

4.3.1 Mean number of Manner-matches and Path-matches across 5 participant groups

The overt choices of participants were determined by the given key ('A' or 'L' covered with a white sticker) that they pressed down during the experiment. All choices were sorted into two categories: Manner-match and Path-match. The group mean was determined by calculating the number of matches out of 16 test items. Figure 1, below, represents the mean number of Manner- and Path-matches across participant groups.

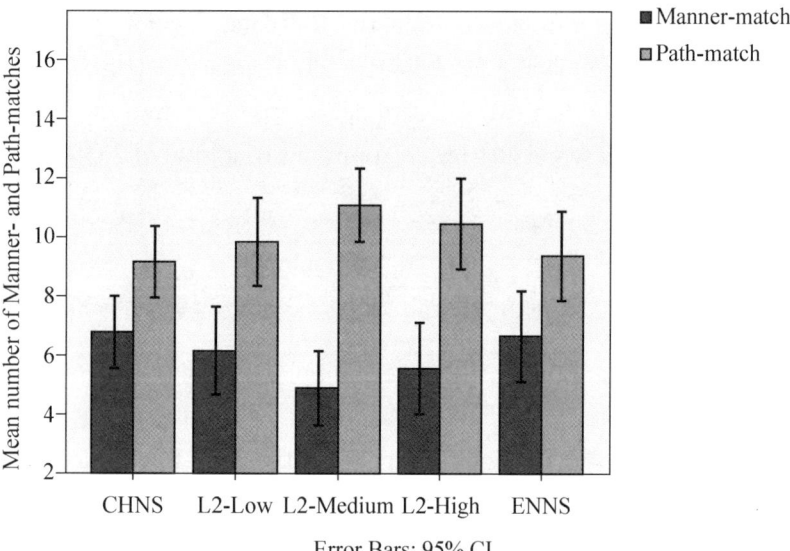

Figure 1 Mean number of Manner- and Path-matches across 5 participant groups

A visual inspection of Figure 1 seems to suggest that native speakers of both English and Chinese, and L2 learners of English, prefer the Path-match over the Manner-match. To verify this observation, t tests were conducted separately in each participant group (CHNS, L2-Low, L2-Medium, L2-High and ENNS). This confirmed that participants' preferences for the Path-match significantly exceeded the chance level (i.e. Table 2).

Table 2 Mean numbers of Manner- vs. Path-matches in 5 participant groups

Group	Mean number of Manner-match (SD)	Mean number of Path-match (SD)	t value	p value
CHNS	6.66 (4.17)	9.34 (4.17)	3.852	0.000***
L2-Low	6.16 (4.02)	9.84 (4.02)	5.354	0.000***
L2-Medium	4.94 (3.44)	11.06 (3.44)	9.367	0.000***
L2-High	5.72 (4.37)	10.28 (4.37)	6.725	0.000***
ENNS	6.78 (3.28)	9.22 (3.28)	3.484	0.001***

*** $=p$ <0.001.

Mixed model logistic regression was carried out using R (version 4.3.1) with glmer function in the package lmerTest to obtain parameter estimates. The overt choice of participants was coded as a binomial dependent variable: The preference to the Path-match was coded as '1' and that to the Manner-match was coded as '0'. First of all, five participant groups (CHNS, L2-Low, L2-Medium, L2-High and ENNS) entered into the model as fixed effects, with participants and items as random effects. The results showed no significant differences between CHNS and the other four groups (p s >0.07). Then the group of ENNS and the three L2 learner groups entered into a new model as fixed effects. No differences were detected between ENNS and the three learner groups (p s >0.05), respectively. Finally, a new model revealed that there were no significant differences in terms of preference between any two groups of L2 learners, p s >0.24 (see Table 3).

Table 3 Regression coefficients for the logistic regression mixed model for Path-matches

	Estimated parameter	z-value	Pr	Estimated parameter	z-value	Pr	Estimated parameter	z-value	Pr	Estimated parameter	z-value	Pr
Fixed effects												
Intercept	0.48463	1.397	0.1624	0.4361#	1.237#	0.2162#	0.6970#	1.904#	0.0569#	0.9031#	2.601#	0.0093**,#
ENNS	-0.05854	-0.164	0.8701									
L2-Low	0.19719	0.547	0.5841	0.2565	0.718	0.4727	0.2335	0.603	0.5465	0.2092	0.557	0.5777
L2-High	0.42209	1.166	0.2437	0.4810	1.339	0.1804						
L2-Medium	0.64028	1.773	0.0762	0.7042	1.966	0.0492*	0.4469	1.158	0.2469			
Random effects	Variance	SD		Variance	SD		Variance	SD		Variance	SD	
Subject (intercept)	1.6757	1.2945		1.6559	1.2868		1.9574	1.3991		1.8241	1.3506	
Item (intercept)	0.8898	0.9433		0.9795	0.9897		0.9504	0.9749		0.7782	0.8821	

shows the intercept value in each model.   * =$p<0.05$;   ** =$p<0.01$;   *** =$p<0.001$.

Chapter 4   The Conceptualisation of Voluntary Motion Events in L2 English Learners (Experiment 1)

4.3.2 RT in judgment across 5 groups of participants

Apart from overt choices, the response latency of participants in their judgments was examined using the continuous measurement of RT in ms (see Figure 2 and Table 4).

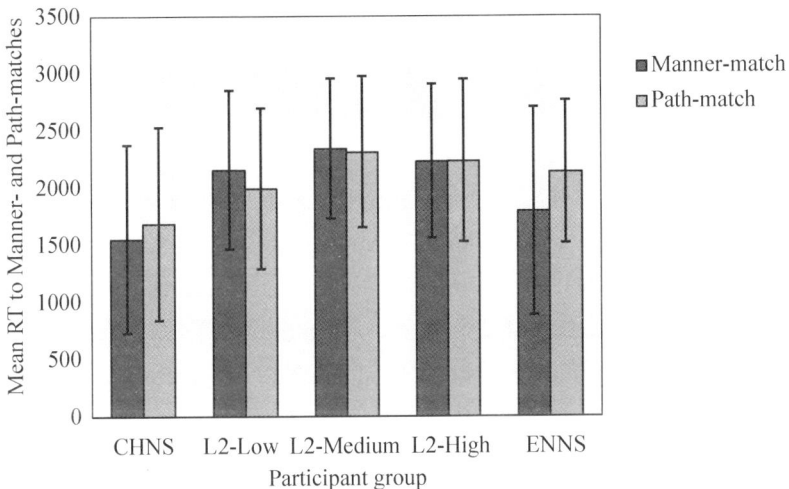

Figure 2   Mean RT (in ms) to Manner- and Path-matches across participant groups

Table 4   Mean RT (in ms) to spontaneous motion scenes in 5 participant groups

Group	Mean overall RT (SD)	Mean RT to Manner-match (SD)	Mean RT to Path-match (SD)
CHNS	1626 (836.33)	1550 (823.16)	1684 (843.26)
L2-Low	2056 (703.32)	2156 (694.47)	1992 (702.81)
L2-Medium	2320 (645.74)	2340 (611.41)	2311 (662.28)
L2-High	2232 (696.23)	2229 (672.21)	2234 (710.20)
ENNS	1996 (770.36)	1792 (907.76)	2136 (623.83)

Generalised linear mixed models regression was carried out using R with lmer function in the package lmerTest to obtain parameter estimates. The best-fit model includes participant group (CHNS, L2-Low, L2-Medium, L2-High and ENNS) and preference type (i.e. Manner-match and Path-match) as fixed effects, with participants and items as random effects. The RT was coded as the dependent variable. The results of the analyses were reported as follows:

a. The overall RT did not vary significantly between the two preference types across all five participant groups ($t = 1.84, p = 0.06$).
b. The overall RT was significantly shorter in the group of CHNS than in the three L2 groups, respectively (p s < 0.001). Then the group of ENNS and the three groups of L2 learners entered into a new model as fixed effects. It was found that the RT in ENNS was significantly shorter than in the three learner groups (p s <0.01). Also, the RT was marginally different between the group of CHNS and that of ENNS ($t = 1.902, p = 0.05$) due to a longer RT in the latter group. In addition, further models revealed no significant differences in RT between the group of L2-High and the other two L2 groups (p s >0.14).
c. More importantly, there was an interaction between the two groups of monolingual speakers and the two preference types. Separate analyses with different models revealed that Chinese monolinguals had a significantly shorter RT to the Path-match than their English counterparts ($t = 4.525, p < 0.001$). Their RT to the Manner-match was also significantly, yet marginally,

different from that of their English peers ($t = 1.974, p = 0.05$).

d. Also, the English monolinguals and the three L2 groups had a significant interaction with the two preference types. Further analyses revealed that English monolinguals had a significantly shorter RT to the Manner-match than the three L2 groups, respectively (p s <0.01). Their RT to the Path-match, however, was comparable with that of the three L2 groups, p s >0.16 (see also Table 5).

4.4 Discussion

The present investigation examines whether, and how, subtle linguistic differences in grammar (as demonstrated in a lexicalisation strategy of motion events) have a mind-shaping effect on the motion event cognition of Chinese-English bilinguals, compared with monolingual speakers. Two sets of data were collected, regarding selection behaviour and implicit processing time, respectively. Our findings are twofold. First of all, for forced choices (i.e. Manner- or Path-matches), there seems to be a shared preference for the Path-matched strategy, irrespective of learner type (L1 vs. L2 speakers) and of proficiency amongst the L2 learners. Secondly, it was found, in the first instance, that for the two groups of L1 learners, the Chinese participants are significantly quicker in automatic processing time than their English counterparts, particularly in judging Path-matched video clips. Further, the L2 learners are found to be generally significantly slower in response time than the two groups of monolingual speakers. In particular, the L2 learners, even at the

Table 5 Regression coefficients for the mixed model for RT to all items

	Estimated parameter	t-value	Pr	Estimated parameter	t-value	Pr	Estimated parameter	t-value	Pr	Estimated parameter	t-value	Pr
Fixed effects												
Intercept	1553.17	18.251	<2e-16***	1761.94#	19.603#	<2e-16***#	2104.50#	21.865#	<2e-16***#	2294.79#	24.105#	<2e-16***#
ENNS	210.25	1.902	0.05828	352.82	3.102	0.0022**	180.55	1.482	0.141	80.026	0.666	0.507
L2-Low	566.10	5.088	6.8e-07***	527.73	4.500	1.1e-05***	258.95	2.141	0.034*	28.546	0.392	0.695
L2-High	731.30	6.338	8.6e-10***	607.03	5.221	4.2e-07***	16.11	0.248	0.804			
L2-Medium	812.58	7.109	8.7e-12***	428.96	6.367	2.5e-10***						
Choice	132.80	1.840	0.06587									
ENNS: Choice	285.75	2.831	0.00468**	-438.42	-4.652	3.6e-06***						
L2-Low: Choice	-158.11	-1.547	0.12207	-400.27	-4.026	5.9e-05***	32.11	0.344	0.731			
L2-High: Choice	-108.66	-1.010	0.31273	-400.28	-4.207	2.7e-05***	31.05	0.348	0.728	-3.294	-0.034	0.972
L2-Medium: Choice	-109.86	-1.064	0.28755									
Random effects	Variance	SD	Variance	SD	Variance	SD	Variance	SD				
Subject (intercept)	108876	330.0		129268	359.5		158151	397.7		140772	375.2	
Item (intercept)	18851	137.3		25848	160.8		33645	183.4		25193	158.7	

shows the intercept value in each model. * =p <0.05; ** =p <0.01; *** =p <0.001.

Chapter 4 The Conceptualisation of Voluntary Motion Events in L2 English Learners (Experiment 1)

advanced stage of acquisition, are reported to be less efficient than monolingual speakers of the target language (i.e. English) in judging Manner-matched scenes, although their reaction time to Path-matched pictures is comparable to that of English monolinguals.

Several observations from our findings deserve a closer examination. First of all, our participants demonstrate a shared orientation towards Path-matches in their overt selections. Such results can be interpreted in quite different ways. It is possible that great variations between languages in motion description tend to be superficial, non-categorical and probabilistic, and do not go beyond the level of language performance to penetrate into the cognitive domain. In other words, linguistic differences in motion description can be regarded, in some sense, as varied instantiations of a common underlying conceptual framework. In light of Talmy's (1985) Path salience hypothesis, Path (rather than Manner) is the most central and indispensable ingredient for any motion event. This may explain why in terms of selection strategy, the participants in our study opt for Path-matches most frequently.

Despite this shared tendency towards the Path dimension, our analysis of RT reveals significant differences between monolingual speakers of different languages, as well as differences between learner types (i.e. L1 vs. L2 learners). Taking into account these observations, it seems more likely that the effect of language typology does exist but fails to be brought forth due to various factors. For instance, the typological distance between equipollently-framed Chinese and satellite-framed English may be too close to allow for any difference in behavioural pattern to surface. In this case, future studies involving an additional verb-framed language, such as Spanish or French, may illustrate the issue more clearly. Also, the measurement of categorical preferences might be too 'coarse' to bring forth any variation in behavioural pattern resulting from minimal differences between languages in motion description. Seen this way, the finer and more subtle measure at the automatic implicit level of conceptualisation (i.e. RT) help reveal a degree of difference in thought pattern that has remained elusive under the categorical gauge.

In addition, there is a third likelihood that the potential language effect has been cancelled or nullified by the verbal interference task utilised in the nonlinguistic experiment. This possibility is in line with the notion that speakers of satellite-framed languages are more likely than those of verb-framed languages to base their similarity judgments on the Manner dimension in the experimental situation, as found in previous studies. However, when the recruitment of languages was hindered through verbal interference, crosslinguistic differences disappear (Montero-Melis & Bylund, 2016; see also Athanasopoulos *et al.*, 2015a).

The second issue meriting further exploration is the significantly shorter RT of Chinese monolingual speakers compared with their English counterparts. Such a phenomenon can be approached from varied perspectives, and the most plausible explanation may follow the argument below. Path is an attribute prominently marked in Chinese but not in English, whereas Manner is prominently marked in both languages. This means that Chinese monolinguals, in contrast with their English counterparts, attend more strongly to Path of motion, develop a cognitive pattern in which Path is given greater prominence than in English, and respond more quickly to the Path attribute of motion events in categorisation or judgment (see similar findings in Kersten *et al.*, 2010). This explains, at least partly, why the RT to the Path-match is exceptionally significantly shorter in Chinese than in English monolinguals.

Chapter 4   The Conceptualisation of Voluntary Motion Events in L2 English Learners (Experiment 1)

The overall RT of the three groups of L2 learners is significantly slower than monolingual speakers of both languages. In particular, they are less efficient in judging Manner-matched scenes compared with the speakers of the target language (i.e. English monolinguals), even at the advanced stage of acquisition. As proposed by Pavlenko (2011), learning an additional language involves a process of conceptual adjustment or switch, for instance, a process of converging L1 and L2 categories or perspectives. Results, as such, seem to suggest that a shift in perspective, for instance shifting from a conceptual pattern in which Manner and Path have equal prominence (i.e. Chinese) to a cognitive mode in which Manner has a greater prominence (i.e. English) can be both cognitively demanding and time-consuming.

Our findings for L2 learners are not consistent with those in some previous studies. Research in bilingual cognitive development has provided evidence that bilingualism can extend one's cognitive capacities. Bilingual speakers are found to outperform their monolingual peers in nonverbal cognitive tasks involving control processes, such as selective attention to given aspects of a problem, inhabitation of attention to irrelevant information and switching between competing alternatives (Kharkhurin, 2010: 213; see also Bialystok, 2009). In particular, investigations suggest that bilingual young adults are significantly quicker in RT than monolingual speakers to 'solve the conflict between the target stimulus and the to-be-ignored flanker information' (e.g. Costa *et al.*, 2008). The task presented in our study (i.e. similarity judgment) is a type of categorisation task in which participants are forced to choose between Manner similarity and Path resemblance. This involves a process by which detectably different stimuli have to be represented as identical in a given aspect, that is, a process requiring attention control to inhibit competing information (i.e. an 'either A or B' choice). Bilinguals who have two languages at their control and who frequently exercise language switch should possess cognitive skills that can either enhance their problem-solving skills as required in the present task or expedite their speed in problem solving.

Despite such potential cognitive advantages, the bilinguals in this study are not comparable to their monolingual counterparts in terms of response latency. It is suggested that such a phenomenon can be approached by taking into consideration some (extra)linguistic factors. Pavlenko (2011) proposes several variables contributing to the attainment of an L2 learner in conceptual restructuring, which involve the age of L2 acquisition, the context of acquisition, the length of exposure to the target language, language proficiency and the frequency of target language use (2011: 249-251). In this light, the Chinese-English bilinguals in our study are largely disadvantaged. To illustrate, these Chinese learners started their English learning around the age of 10 - 12. As reported by Hohenstein *et al.* (2006), speakers who acquire their L2 before the age of 5 are more likely to display target-like responses in linguistic and behavioural tasks than those who start L2 learning at a later stage of acquisition (e.g. after 12 years old). In terms of the language-learning context, the L2 learners in the present study live in a predominately Chinese-speaking environment where they use only Chinese in their daily life. Their English input is rather limited and mainly comes from classroom teaching, which averages about four hours per week. Previous research has revealed that immersion in an L2 context facilitates conceptual restructuring; years of immersion create a more reliable predictor of target-like behaviour than years of formal instruction (see Pavlenko, 2011: 250 for a summary of relevant findings). None of the bilinguals in our study, however, had the experience of visiting

Chapter 4 The Conceptualisation of Voluntary Motion Events in L2 English Learners (Experiment 1)

or living in an English-speaking country for a period of longer than two weeks. Furthermore, they used English at a very low frequency and mainly in English classroom activities. Seen this way, it is understandable that the RT evidence in the present study suggests that these bilinguals are in a stage of on-going restructuring of their conceptual frameworks.

Our research findings are generally in line with the results from investigations of L2 linguistic encoding of motion events, particularly those involving an acquisition of advanced linguistic skills, such as syntactic organisation and discourse strategy. To cite an example, Ji & Hohenstein (2014a, 2014b) systematically investigate how English learners of Chinese syntactically package varied semantic components for complex caused motion events (e.g. Manner, Cause, Path, etc.). It is reported that even the advanced L2 learners have not fully acquired the typical syntactic pattern in motion description in the target language. They have arrived, instead, at an inter-language, showing some resemblance to the target system as well as some traces of L1 influence. Furthermore, no developmental tendency was observed at the initial and intermediate stages of acquisition; non-significant changes occurred only when learners progressed to an advanced level. Taken together, findings in L2 motion representation, at both linguistic and conceptual levels, suggest a general difficulty in fully adapting to the target pattern in L2 learners. Seen in this way, these results seem to be consistent with a weak version of the linguistic relativity hypothesis. In Slobin's 'thinking for speaking' hypothesis, he argues that a native language 'is not a neutral coding system of an objective reality', but instead is a system that has trained its speakers from early on to pay attention to specific aspects of events and experience when talking about them (Slobin, 1996: 89). 'Thinking for speaking' involves picking those characteristics of objects and events that simultaneously fit some conceptualisation of the event and are readily encodable in the language (Slobin, 1996: 75-76). In this sense, one's thinking for speaking pattern, which is ingrained from the childhood, should be particularly resistant to remoulding in adult L2 acquisition.

The linguistic and conceptual representation of motion events in the L2 domain is a complex issue, involving multiple factors to weigh at the same time. Findings from previous investigations seem varied. On the one hand, much research detected the effects of L1 on linguistic expression and on the conceptualisation of motion events in L2 learners, particularly in those of low proficiency. On the other, behavioural and neurophysiological evidence reveals that human linguistic and cognitive systems can be highly adaptive and flexible. Some key questions need to be addressed in future studies in the domain of bilingual cognition. These include: which aspect(s) of language (e.g. grammatical aspect, lexicalisation) affects which part of the cognitive system in L2 learners (e.g. sensory perception, object categorisation)? What is the exact mechanism that determines the extent and nature of cognitive restructuring in L2 learners? What is the relative weight of the varied linguistic and sociocultural factors that modulate the effect of bilingualism on cognition?

Chapter 5
The Conceptualisation of Caused Motion Events in L2 English Learners (Experiment 2)

The experiment is generally interested in two questions:

a. Whether the effect of motion language typology can go beyond language performance, and influence motion conceptualisation of monolingual speakers (as tested in a triads matching task);
b. Whether, and how, the motion conceptualisation of L2 learners differs from that of monolinguals. Does the behavioural evidence suggest any significant shift in conceptualisation patterns across proficiencies?

This study thus compares, in the first instance, how different types of speakers (L1 vs. L2 learners; English monolinguals vs. Chinese monolinguals, L2 learners at different proficiencies) evaluate the similarity between motion screens (as indicated by their overt preferences), and the extent to which their decision strategies can be considered language-biased. Further, it investigates whether there is any difference in response latency (as measured by RT) in judgment across different types of speakers, and the extent to which L2 learners' efficiency in reaction is comparable to that of source (or target) language speakers.

With respect to research methodologies, this investigation followed the principles as elaborated in Chapter 4 in aspects such as recruiting participants, administering pretest and testing procedures, and coding behavioural data (See Section 4.2).

5.1 Research questions and hypotheses

We generate three hypotheses regarding the research questions. First of all, at one extreme, a 'universal' prediction might be made in which language-specific influence is only superficial and cannot go deeper into the cognitive level. Following Talmy's (2000) 'basic motion scheme' and the universal cognitive salience of Path (vs. Manner) in the human mind, different types of speakers may prefer the Path-match over the Manner-match more frequently in their judgments.

Secondly, at the other extreme, we hypothesize a strong effect of linguistic relativity, in which the behaviour of different types of speakers can be largely predicted by relevant language differences. Due to the high 'codability' of Manner information in the linguistic encoding of motion events in English and its psychological implications (i.e. more habitual attention to Manner dimension), we predict that English monolinguals would be more Manner-oriented than their Chinese counterparts in more frequently preferring the Manner-matches (i.e. less frequently preferring the Path-matches) and reacting significantly more quickly in Manner-matched decisions than in Path-matched choices. Following the main arguments of linguistic relativity, speakers have been trained, since childhood, to think in a way that is largely constrained by their native language; their particular way of thinking should be rather hard to remould in adulthood. We thus predict that L2 learners at low and/or

Chapter 5 The Conceptualisation of Caused Motion Events in L2 English Learners (Experiment 2)

intermediate proficiencies should show behavioural evidence of being more native-language biased; only at an advanced stage of acquisition would it be likely that Chinese learners of L2 English behave in a more target-language biased way.

Previous findings suggest that L2 learners may demonstrate a U-shaped curve across three proficiencies in restructuring their construal of particular types of motion events, for example in studies focusing on a contrast between boundedness vs. unboundedness in aspect. Low-level learners can change their motion event cognitive representations at the initial stage because their system is affected at a general level by statistical learning (similar to the effects of laboratory training). Learners at the intermediate level may seem to revert back to a native-language biased pattern; however, at a fine-grained level of cognition, they undergo a process of suppression (of routinized L1 categorisation pattern) and internalisation (of a novel event construal). Only learners of high proficiencies are reported to have shifted completely towards an L2 cognitive pattern (Athanasopoulos et al., 2015b: 148-149 for a detailed discussion). The inclusion of three proficiencies in the present study thus aims to reveal clearly any developmental trajectory (linear or nonlinear) in cognitive representations of motion events focusing on a comparison between satellite-framedness and equipollently-framedness.

Thirdly, similarity judgments of participants will be assessed by both categorical measurement (i.e. overt preferences) and continuous measurement (i.e. RT). The former variable can only answer the dichotomous question of whether language influences nonverbal cognition (i.e. A or B in a forced similarity judgment task), whilst the latter variable allows us to test the degree of differences (if any) in behaviour as engendered by language differences. Given the fact that the two languages under investigation are only partially different (rather than entirely opposing), there is a third likelihood, in which the proportion of overt preferences for Manner (or Path) might not vary significantly across types of participants; any language-biased patterns in behaviour will only be evident (if at all) when examined under the lens of RT.

Clearly, decision and RT are two different types of data, and the latter can reveal aspects of processing that are often not available in results from choice response measures. According to Tokowicz and MacWhinney (2005), certain measurements such as event-related potential (ERP) and RT can directly reflect automatic, non-reflective, implicit responses to stimuli. We thus reason that any differences in RT between Manner- vs. Path-match in our study would reflect online implicit processing, and that overt Manner- or Path-matched choices would reflect primarily explicit processing. Previous literature suggests that there is often a divergence between explicit and implicit measures of L2 learning, which may be due to the behavioural task demand.

To illustrate, Li *et al.* (1993) investigate how participants interpret sentences in a language without inflections (i.e. Chinese) by using other types of linguistic cues (such as word order and noun animacy). Chinese L2 learners hear a sentence played back on a speaker and simultaneously see on the computer screen a pair of pictures that correspond to the two objects described in the sentence. They are then asked to decide which of the two objects in the pictures is the doer of the action in the sentence by indicating their choice on a button box. It is reported that although the final choice decisions for two different sentences may be the same, the amount of time it takes to reach the same decision is very different, showing clear effects of linguistic cues with varying degrees of strength in the interpretation process. Although the current study focuses on motion

Chapter 5 The Conceptualisation of Caused Motion Events in L2 English Learners (Experiment 2)

animations, not sentence interpretation, we believe that the two tasks recruit the same mental format that codes the interpretation, rather than the perceptual properties of sentences or pictures/videos. In other words, both tasks involve thought processes that are cognitive in nature and deal with interpreted knowledge (see Clark & Chase [1972] for a detailed discussion). In this light, we include in our study the continuous measurement of RT and compare it with the behavioural data with the aim of providing a more sensitive method for measuring implicit processing.

5.2 Materials

Forty-eight short video clips (five seconds each) were used as our stimuli, each depicting a caused motion event, in which both Manner (coupled with Cause) and Path were presented as equally salient. These stimuli conformed to previous models of caused motion developed by Hickmann *et al.* (2009): both presented a specific type of caused motion, in which an agent carried out a specific action to an object, which changed its location due to the external force; meanwhile, the agent accompanied the moving object (by *walking*) throughout its course of movement. All stimuli illustrated six specific types of Manner (*pushing / pulling, rolling / sliding, throwing / kicking*) and eight types of Path: verticality (*up* and *down*), boundary crossing (*across* and *into*), deixis (*towards* and *away from*) and trajectory parallel to, or encircling, the Ground (*along* and *around*). To illustrate, the target scene in triad 2 in Appendix B depicted a boy (Bonny) pulling a treasure bag up a pyramid, the bag sliding up the pyramid and the boy accompanying the bag all the way to the top of the pyramid.

A total of 48 motion video clips were organised into a set of 16 triads: 16 targets and 32 alternates (two for each of the target events). Target and alternate videos appeared for 5 seconds each and were then followed by 1 second of black screen. The task lasted approximately 6 minutes in total. All stimuli were arranged into two randomised orders: A and B (A reversed). These orders were counterbalanced across participants within group. The presentation position of Manner-matched vs. Path-matched video clips (left side or right side of the screen) was counterbalanced across stimuli in a given order.

Within a triad, the target video clip depicted the boy performing a specific action which caused the movement of an object (e.g. pulling a treasure bag up the pyramid), while the two alternate video clips showed the same boy involved in similar actions with changes in either Manner or Path. In the Path-match alternate, the Path of motion remained the same while the Manner of motion was changed (e.g. *pushing* a treasure bag up the pyramid), while in the Manner-match alternate, the Path varied with Manner kept the same (e.g. pulling a treasure bag *into* the pyramid). In order to direct the participants' attention to the similarity between actions rather than anything else, all stimuli involved the same boy with the same clothing. In each triad, the background scenery for motion was also kept uniform across the target and two alternates. An example of caused motion stimuli with coloured illustration is provided in Appendix B.

5.3 Results

This section reports findings in relation to two main questions: a) whether participants' behavioural responses vary significantly with group (i.e. CHNS, L2-Low, L2-Medium, L2-High, ENNS) and/or with preference type (i.e. Manner-match and Path-match); b) whether the overall RT to caused motion stimuli varies significantly as a function of participant group and/or preference type. Depending on specific questions asked, statistical tests, such as two-way mixed analysis of variance (ANOVA), were utilised to explore relevant datasets.

5.3.1 *Number of Manner- and Path-matched judgments across 5 participant groups*

The preferences of the participants were decided according to the specific key ('A' or 'L' on the keyboard) they signalled while judging the similarity between motion screens. The data was thus represented as falling into one of the two major strategies: the Manner-match or the Path-match. The mean was calculated by recording the number of matches out of 16 individuals in a group. Figure 3, below, presents the mean number of both Manner-matched and Path-matched preferences across five participant groups (CHNS, L2-Low, L2-Medium, L2-High and ENNS). There seemed to be a shared tendency for the Path-match over the Manner-match across groups.

A two-way mixed ANOVA with participant group (CHNS, L2-Low, L2-Medium, L2-High and ENNS) as the between subjects factor, and preference type (Manner-match, Path-match) as a within-subjects factor revealed a main effect of preference only, $F(4, 155) = 90.204$, $p < 0.001$, $\eta 2 = 0.368$. The total mean number of Path-matches ($M = 10.556$) significantly exceeded that of Manner-matches ($M = 5.444$, $p < 0.001$). No interaction effect between group and

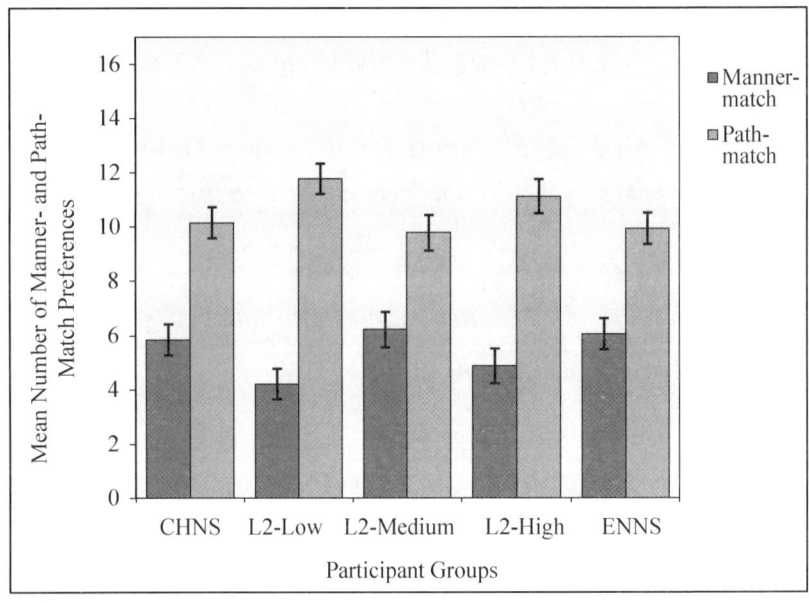

Figure 3 Mean number of Manner-matched and Path-matched preferences across 5 participant groups

error bars indicate mean ± SE

preference type was observed, $F_{(4, 155)} = 2.048$, ns [1]. A closer look at the data further indicated that the mean number of Path-matched preferences reached significantly above average (i.e. 8 out of 16 matches) in all five groups: CHNS: $M = 10.16$ ($SD = 3.254$), 95% CI [8.98, 11.33]; L2-Low: $M = 11.78$ ($SD = 3.160$), 95% CI [10.64, 12.92]; L2-Medium: $M = 9.78$ ($SD = 3.705$), 95% CI

---

[1] The effect of the 'group' variable was not computed in two-way ANOVAs in this sub-section because there were no missing values in relevant datasets and the total number of preferences (i.e. both Manner- and Path-matches) remained as a constant across participants, groups and items.

[8.45, 11.12]; L2-High: $M = 11.13$ ($SD = 3.617$), 95% CI [9.82, 12.43] and ENNS: $M = 9.94$ ($SD = 3.252$), 95% CI [8.76, 11.11]. These results disconfirmed one of our hypotheses regarding a possible strong effect of linguistic relativity; English monolinguals did not prefer the Path-match significantly less frequently than their Chinese counterparts.

A different perspective was taken on these results by conducting a by-item analysis on the choices. A two-way repeated measures ANOVA with group (CHNS, L2-Low, L2-Medium, L2-High, ENNS) and preference type (Manner-match, Path-match) as two within-items factors revealed, first of all, a main effect of preference, $F(4, 60) = 8.591$, $p = 0.01$, partial $\eta 2 = 0.364$. The total mean number of Path-matches ($M = 21.125$) significantly exceeded that of Manner-matches ($M = 10.875$, $p < 0.01$). Meanwhile, the analysis showed a significant interaction between group and preference, $F(4, 60) = 8.266$, $p < 0.001$, partial $\eta 2 = 0.355$. Pairwise comparisons with Bonferroni correction confirmed that the differences in the total mean number of Path-matches vs. Manner-matches were significant in monolingual speakers of Chinese (CHNS: mean difference = 8.625, $p = 0.033$, partial $\eta 2 = 0.270$), L2 learners of low proficiency (L2-Low: mean difference $=15.125$, $p = 0.001$, partial $\eta 2 = 0.541$) and those at the advanced level of acquisition (L2-High: mean difference $=12.500$, $p = 0.001$, partial $\eta 2 = 0.525$). There was a trend towards a significant difference in the total mean number of Path-matches vs. Manner-matches in L2 learners of medium proficiency (L2-Medium: mean difference $=7.25$, $p = 0.064$) and monolingual speakers of English (ENNS: mean difference $=7.75$, $p = 0.061$). Thus, the two sets of analyses (i.e. by participant and by item) roughly converge on differences arising between the Path-match and the Manner-match.

5.3.2 RT in Manner- and Path-matched judgments across 5 participant groups

In this sub-section, we investigated whether the overall RT to video clips varied significantly with participant group and/or preference type. A by-participant mixed ANOVA was performed in the first instance, which was followed by a by-item repeated measures ANOVA.

A two-way mixed ANOVA was first conducted with group (CHNS, L2-Low, L2-Medium, L2-High, ENNS) as the between subjects factor and preference type (Manner-match, Path-match) as a within subjects factor. It revealed a statistically significant main effect for participant group, $F(4, 155) = 6.853$, $p < 0.001$, partial $\eta 2 = 0.150$, as well as a statistically significant main effect for preference type, $F(1, 155) = 11.413$, $p = 0.001$, partial $\eta 2 = 0.069$. Furthermore, a statistically significant interaction between group and preference type was attested, $F(4, 155) = 2.756$, $p = 0.030$, partial $\eta 2 = 0.066$ (see Figure 4).

Pairwise comparisons with Bonferroni adjustment were used to further examine the interaction between participant group and mean RT to Manner- vs. Path-match. These analyses indicated that differences in the mean RT to Manner- vs. Path-matched conditions were statistically significant for monolingual speakers of English (ENNS: mean difference $= -210$, $p = 0.033$, partial $\eta 2 = 0.029$), L2 learners of high proficiency (L2-High: mean difference $= -368$, $p < 0.001$, partial $\eta 2 = 0.084$) and those at the intermediate level (L2-Medium: mean difference $= -214$, $p = 0.029$, partial $\eta 2 = 0.030$). However, the RT to Manner- vs. Path-matched conditions was approximately equivalent for monolingual speakers of Chinese

Chapter 5 The Conceptualisation of Caused Motion Events in L2 English Learners (Experiment 2)

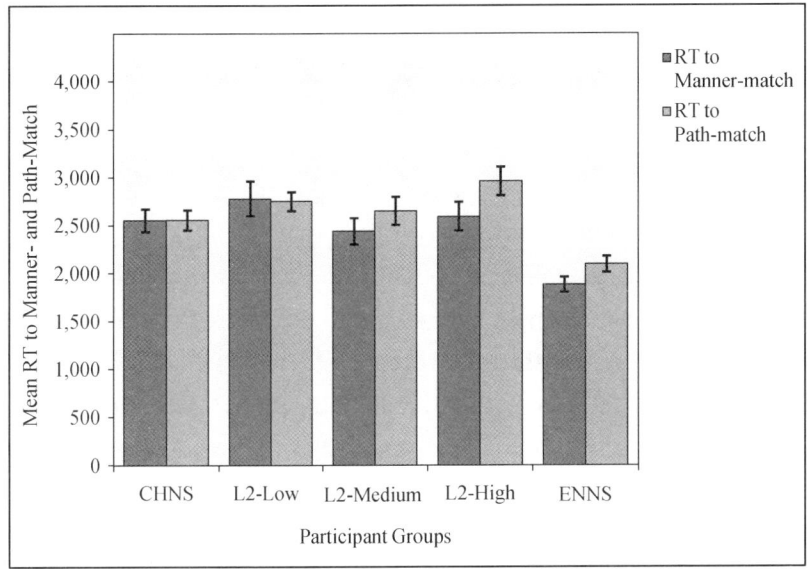

Figure 4 The mean RT (in ms) to Manner- vs. Path-matches across participant groups

error bars indicate mean ± SE

(CHNS: mean difference = −4, *ns*) and L2 learners at the initial stage of their acquisition (L2-Low: mean difference =28, *ns*; see also Table 6).

Table 6 RT (in ms) in Manner-matched and Path-matched conditions across participant groups

Participant Groups	Mean RT in Manner-match	Mean RT in Path-match
CHNS	2553 (*SD* =674)	2557 (*SD* =602)
L2-Low	2780 (*SD* =1028)	2752 (*SD* =559)
L2-Medium	2437 (*SD* =784)	2652 (*SD* =838)
L2-High	2593 (*SD* =858)	2961 (*SD* =832)
ENNS	1883 (*SD* =477)	2093 (*SD* =472)

As mentioned earlier, the two-way mixed ANOVA confirmed that, generally, English speakers were significantly quicker in responding to caused motion stimuli in their similarity judgments, as compared to all other 4 groups (i.e. the main effect of group). A closer examination of the dataset via multiple comparisons with Bonferroni correction further revealed that in making Manner-matched choices, monolingual speakers of English were significantly quicker than their Chinese peers (mean difference = − 670, p = 0.008), as well as the three L2 groups (ENNS vs. L2-Low: mean difference = − 897, p < 0.001; ENNS vs. L2-Medium: mean difference = − 555, p = 0.052, and ENNS vs. L2-High: mean difference = − 710, p = 0.004). By contrast, in opting for Path-matched motion scenes, monolingual speakers of English did not differ significantly from their Chinese counterparts (mean difference = − 464, ns), though they still reacted quicker as compared to the learner groups (ENNS vs. L2-Low: mean difference = − 659, p = 0.001; ENNS vs. L2-Medium: mean difference = − 559, p = 0.012, and ENNS vs. L2-High: mean difference = − 868, p < 0.001). Such a contrast in RT between the two groups of monolingual speakers is of particular importance in indicating that the overall quicker RT of English monolinguals can be attributed to their even quicker reaction to Manner-matches.

Secondly, an additional by-item analysis was further performed on the RT data to investigate whether the interaction effect between participant group and preference type remains systematic across individual items. A two-way repeated measures ANOVA with group (CHNS, L2-Low, L2-Medium, L2-High, ENNS) and preference type (Manner-match, Path-match) as two within-items factors showed a main effect of group, $F(4, 60) = 40.119, p < 0.001$, partial $\eta^2 = 0.728$, as well as a marginally statistically significant effect of preference type, $F(1, 15) = 4.262$, $p = 0.057$, partial $\eta 2 = 0.221$. Meanwhile, the test revealed a significant interaction between group and preference, $F(4, 60) = 2.901$, $p = 0.029$, partial $\eta 2 = 0.162$. Pairwise comparisons with Bonferroni correction further revealed that the differences in mean RT between Manner- vs. Path-match were significant in monolingual speakers of English (ENNS: mean difference $= -336$, $p = 0.011$, partial $\eta 2 = 0.358$) and L2 learners of high proficiency (L2-High: mean difference $= -433$, $p = 0.036$, partial $\eta 2 = 0.262$). However, no difference was detected for the group of monolingual speakers of Chinese (CHNS: mean difference $= 0.128$, ns), as well as L2 learners at low and intermediate levels (L2-Low: mean difference $= 27$, ns; L2-Medium: mean difference $= -283$, ns).

In summary, our by-participant and by-item analyses converge on an observation that the differences in RT to Manner-match vs. Path-match vary significantly, depending on participant group. Great discrepancies were attested between typologically different L1s (English vs. Chinese), different learner types (monolinguals vs. L2 learners), and across different proficiencies amongst L2 learners (Low and/or Medium vs. High). Monolingual speakers of English reacted significantly quicker to the Manner-match than to the Path-match, whereas their Chinese counterparts used an approximately equal amount of time in making Manner- and Path-matched decisions. As for L2 learners, they seem to achieve a target language-biased cognitive pattern only at a relatively advanced stage of acquisition.

5.4 Discussion

The current chapter investigates how Chinese learners of English at different proficiencies conceptualise motion in a triads matching task, as compared to monolingual speakers of English and Chinese. Two main questions are asked: a) whether the effect of motion language typology can go beyond language performance and influence nonverbal event categorisation of monolingual speakers; b) whether, and how, the nonverbal event categorisation of L2 learners differs from that of monolinguals and, further, whether there are any significant shifts in motion cognition pattern across proficiencies, as suggested by the behavioural evidence. Overall, our two sets of analyses (i.e. categorisation preferences and RT data) produce seemingly conflicting results. In terms of choice response, both monolinguals of different languages and L2 learners at varied proficiencies prefer the Path-matched screens in judgment. However, in terms of RT, English monolinguals, as well as medium and/or high proficiency L2 learners, respond more efficiently to Manner-matched (vs. Path-matched) motion stimuli than Chinese monolinguals, and low-level L2 learners. It merits mentioning that such significant differences in RT across five groups are obtained in a truly 'non-linguistic' context (i.e. the 'number-shadowing' procedure). Given that the effect of linguistic relativity is normally cancelled in verbal interference tasks as revealed in some previous studies (e.g. Athanasopoulos *et al.*, 2015a; Gennari *et al.*, 2002; Papafragou *et al.*, 2002), the set of findings regarding the RT data is of particular significance in suggesting that the effects of language may be strong enough to lead to variations in nonverbal categorisation of motion events even in the presence of verbal interference.

The first question arising from the above reported findings may be why Chinese and English monolinguals did not show any significant variations in their choice response, despite the striking differences in linguistic encoding of motion events between these two languages. Such an observation may be interpreted from different

Chapter 5 The Conceptualisation of Caused Motion Events in L2 English Learners (Experiment 2)

perspectives. One possibility, as suggested by Lupyan (2012), is that describing events constitutes an inherently more complex form of linguistic labelling than, say, object naming. Therefore, any widely attested differences in motion description across world languages tend to be probabilistic rather than categorical, showing great within-language variability. As a case in point, French is traditionally and standardly considered as a verb-framed language, but recent studies reveal that apart from expressing Path of motion in the verb, French can also express Path in a prefix demonstrating a satellite-framed pattern with high degree of productivity (Kopecka, 2006: 85-91). The implication of such observations is that due to this variability within language, habitual language experience 'might not bias speakers of different languages to distinct event components in a categorical way, which, in turn, would limit the cross-linguistic differences one should expect in nonverbal tasks' (see Montero-Melis, 2016: 642 for a detailed discussion).

Note that our results regarding the choice data are inconsistent with findings of some previous studies using similar triads matching tasks in relation to motion events. To illustrate, Athanasopoulos *et al.* (2015b) report that English (an aspect language) focuses on the 'ongoingness' of events whereas German (a nonaspect language) emphasizes on the 'end point/goal' of motion. Such a crosslinguistic difference is found to influence the nonverbal event categorisation of native speakers of the two languages. German monolinguals tend to base their judgments on endpoint saliency whereas their English peers prefer to select on the basis of 'ongoingness'. The discrepancy between present results for the choices and those in the study of Athanasopoulos *et al.* (2015b) may be attributable, in the first instance, to the absence of verbal interference in the latter study in which participants may have subconsciously used the linguistic clues to aid their judgments①.

A more important reason for the discrepancy, however, might be related to the degree of differences between the two languages under comparison in given aspects. In Athanasopoulos et al.'s (2015b) study, there seems to be a black-and-white contrast between English and German in terms of grammatical aspect (i.e. [+aspect] vs. [- aspect]). Such a stark contrast does not hold between Chinese and English (and in general, between equipollently- and satellite-framed languages) in terms of Manner and Path salience. In both languages, the Manner information is highlighted in the marked grammatical category of verb (in verb root in English and in compound verb in Chinese). The Path dimension is characteristically encoded in both languages as well though its salience is accentuated in varying degrees: it is encoded in the grammatically marked category of verb in Chinese but outside the verbal domain in unmarked categories of particles and prepositions in English. Put another way, Manner and Path salience is essentially a matter of degree (rather than an 'either Manner or Path' distinction) in the current investigation. In English, although Manner is linguistically presented as more salient than Path, such relative salience is not sufficiently strong to exert a categorical impact on nonverbal behaviour, say, leading to a preference for the

---

① In a similar study conducted by Athanasopoulos et al. (2015a), the crosslinguistic differences between English and German in terms of grammatical aspect are reported to disappear in nonverbal event categorisation in the presence of verbal interference. Participants of both language groups show a preference for motion ongoingness, probably because in both the target scene and the ongoingness alternates, the endpoint is not reached (see Athanasopoulos et al., 2015a: 523 for a detailed discussion).

Chapter 5 The Conceptualisation of Caused Motion Events in L2 English Learners (Experiment 2)

Manner-matched scenes amongst English monolinguals. Given that Path (rather than Manner) is the only indispensable and universally salient ingredient for any motion event (see Talmy's [2000] 'basic motion scheme'), it is little wonder that Chinese and English monolinguals behave similarly in their overt choices (i.e. a shared preference for the Path-match) in the current experimental scheme.

The above discussions highlight the importance of introducing the RT data into our analysis: they may be more sensitive to language effects that are too probabilistic to detect in the choice response in a forced similarity judgment context. In hindsight, the adoption of RT in measuring the implicit processing in similarity judgments is particularly useful to our study. Overt choices (i.e. Manner- or Path-match) reveal information about what decisions participants make, and how often they make it, whilst the RT provides information about the speed with which participants render a judgment. Given that the two sets of measurements produce findings that are inconsistent with each other, the RT data aids us in revealing aspects of processing that are not readily available in choice results.

RT is traditionally defined as a measure of the time it takes people to retrieve information from memory (Collins & Quillian, 1969). Questions arise as to what information has been retrieved in context, as presented in the current experimental design. Given the universal cognitive salience of Path for motion event conceptualisation (Talmy's [2000] 'basic motion scheme') and the high 'codability' of Manner in both Chinese and English, it is highly likely that both Manner and Path dimensions are retrieved by participants in the judgment process. The real difference between monolingual speakers of Chinese and English lies in the way that retrieved information has been processed prior to rendering a judgment. Given that Manner and Path receive equal salience in Chinese, it seems plausible to assume that these two dimensions are processed in a 'parallel' fashion, that is, Chinese monolinguals weigh simultaneously the salience of Manner vs. Path before they arrive at a conclusion. By contrast, native speakers of English may have attended to the Manner dimension for judgment in the first instance. In actual behaviour, although they mostly prefer the Path-match, when they do choose the Manner-match, they are responding particularly quickly. In cases where aspects of the motion stimuli are deemed not sufficiently supportive of a judgment based on Manner-salience, English monolinguals then turn to the Path dimension for further processing. In other words, English monolinguals may probably deal with the retrieved information in a 'sequential' way. Seen in this light, a 'negation' phase seems to exist among English monolinguals between their initial Manner-matched evaluation and the subsequent Path-matched judgment. According to Collins & Quillian (1969), a typical model for Negation Time consists of three phases: reading time (viewing time in our case), encoding time and comparison time (1969: 502). It is reasonable to hypothesize that in reaching a Path-matched decision, an additional process of negation may have prolonged the encoding time, thus resulting in the great discrepancy in RT to Manner- vs. Path-matched videos in English monolinguals.

As for L2 learners, our study suggests that those participants of medium and high proficiencies can reconstruct their motion cognition pattern biased towards the target language in online processing, although the more novice learners still show a native-language biased cognitive mode. Slobin predicts, in his 'thinking for speaking' hypothesis, that learning a second language basically means acquiring an alternative way of thinking, and the L1 'thinking for speaking' pattern, which is ingrained from childhood, is 'exceptionally resistant to reconstructing in adult second language acquisition' (1996: 89). There is already an abundant literature concerning the L2 acquisition of motion description, mostly confirming that L2 learners are able to shake off the constraints of their L1 linguistic pattern and get acclimatised to the target language-biased pattern whilst speaking an L2. This even occurs when L1 and L2 are typologically opposing or the linguistic pattern to acquire involves complicated and advanced language skills, such as syntactic construction and discourse organisation (Cadierno, 2004; Cadierno & Ruiz, 2006; Ji & Hohenstein, 2014a, b, to name a few). Taken together, our findings seem to suggest that when engaged in online language-recruiting activities (e.g. speaking, listening, translating) or in nonverbal behavioural tasks, an individual's motion event cognition pattern might not be as resistant to remoulding as is previously proposed.

Having said that, one should bear in mind that in our particular experimental context, the languages in comparison are at least partially similar in terms of motion event typology (i.e. both have satellite-framing properties) and motion event representation (i.e. both focus on Manner-salience). Therefore, it sounds plausible to assume that the L2 learners in our task do not have necessarily completed a process of conceptual convergence or switch; instead, in our case, in which the L2 cognitive pattern for motion (i.e. Manner-salience) constitutes a subset of the L1 motion conceptualisation pattern (i.e. both Manner and Path salience), the L2 learners may have simply activated the relevant part of the conceptualisation pattern in their native language in order to utilise it in their implicit processing.

Chapter 6
Conceptualising Motion Events in L2 Chinese Learners (Experiment 3)

In this chapter, we aim to explore how English learners of Chinese, at both low and intermediate-high proficiencies, judge the overall similarity between voluntary and caused motion video clips.

As elaborated in the introductory chapter, English is a typically satellite-framed language with Manner of motion expressed in the main verb and Path in verb particles. The picture of Chinese, however, is quite complicated and remains a hotly disputed issue. It is commonly believed to stand midway along a satellite- vs. verb-framed continuum, and demonstrates systematically both satellite-framing and verb-framing features (Manner in particles, Path in main verb).

As far as linguistic expression of motion is concerned, English learners of Chinese need to move from a rather transparent pattern to a relatively mixed mode. To exemplify, caused motion events in English are expressed via a 'Manner- and Cause-verb + Path particle' combination, whereas in Chinese, at least two syntactic structures can be recruited to encode caused motion: a) the *BA* construction (e. g. *Ta* 1 *ba* 3 *che* 1 *tui* 1 *guo* 4 *ma* 3 *lu* 4 'He pushed the toy car across the street'), or b) the *ZHE* construction (e.g. *Ta* 1 *tui* 1 *zhe che* 1 *guo* 4 *ma* 3 *lu* 4 'He, pushing the toy car, went across the street'). If we temporarily agree with Talmy (1985) and take the second constituent in the resultative verb compound (RVC) (i. e. *guo* 4 'across') as a particle (rather than an independent verb), then English learners of Chinese may just mirror the language pattern for motion expression in their first language L1 (i.e. *push across*) onto the linguistic system of L2 Chinese (i.e. *tui* 1 'push' *guo* 4 'across'), thus adopting the *BA* construction (rather than the *ZHE* construction) frequently. Seen this way, in encoding motion events, English is a language that provides 'unambiguous' structure (i.e. verb + particle), whereas in Chinese, the relevant language structure is 'ambiguous' in the sense that there exist at least two standard structures to encode the same event (i.e. *BA* and *ZHE*; theory of Structural Ambiguity [Muller, 1998]). The language pattern in English thus stresses on Manner of motion since this information is encoded in the arguably more important grammatical category of the main verb, thus helping to foster a habitual attention to the Manner dimension on the part of its speakers (i.e. Manner salience in English). In contrast, the compound verb (RVC) in Chinese encoded Manner and Path simultaneously in the verb, and sometimes even Path alone in the main verb (as is the case of *ZHE* construction with a single Path verb like *guo* 4 'cross', *shang* 4 'ascend', etc.). By this it is meant that Chinese speakers may develop a habitual attention to Manner and Path simultaneously in their motion event cognition (i.e. Manner + Path salience). From the perspective of conceptual transfer, English learners of Chinese need to recalibrate their L1 thinking pattern and acquire a new pattern of conceptualisation in which Path is attached greater prominence. This may create greater cognitive load on L2 learners, thus exerting important influence on the rate and progress of their conceptual restructuring.

Given the context of this study and relevant previous findings, we make the following predictions regarding the behaviour of L2

Chinese learners in nonlinguistic tasks such as the similarity judgment in our case: a. In terms of preferences, monolingual speakers of Chinese and English, as well as L2 learners across proficiencies, will tend to prefer the Path-match over the Manner-match. b. In terms of RT, Chinese monolingual speakers will use shorter time in their judgment as they may process Manner and Path dimensions simultaneously. English speakers may react quicker to the Manner dimension in their evaluation since they are more habituated to it. Taking into the account the differences between thinking patterns in Chinese and English, and the associated cognitive load in conceptual transfer, it is hypothesized that L2 learners, particularly those at low-intermediate levels, will behave like the speakers of their L1. Only at the advanced level will L2 speakers show signs of conceptual transfer and resemble the target population in terms of RT pattern.

6.1 Research methodologies

A total of 115 students participated in this study. They were divided into 4 groups. Thirty-two monolingual speakers of English were recruited through a university in London, UK (Age: $M = 26.00$ years; $SD = 5.17$). Thirty-two Chinese monolingual speakers were selected from a senior vocational high school in Yantai, China (Age: $M = 19.30$ years; $SD = 0.97$). There were also twenty-three L2 learners with high proficiency in Chinese (Age: $M = 26.57$ years, $SD = 4.72$; L2 exposure: 3.85 years) and twenty-eight L2 learners who were beginners in the acquisition of Chinese (Age: $M = 24.43$ years, $SD = 4.29$; L2 exposure: 1.03 years). All L2 learners were recruited from a university in Shenzhen City, China, and they came from countries such as the UK, the US, Australia, Canada and South Africa. The proficiency levels of L2 learners were determined by their test scores in the HSK Tests . As the official measure of Chinese proficiency, these tests distinguish 6 tiers with tier 6 representing the highest level of Chinese proficiency. In this experiment, L2 participants who had scored at tiers 4, 5 and 6 were categorized as English learners of Chinese with intermediate-high proficiency, and those who passed tier 2 or 3 were considered to be L2 learners with low proficiency in Chinese. No participant took the HSK test at tier 1. All L2 learners had taken the HSK tests 6 months or so prior to the experiment.

It is worth mentioning that the group of monolingual speakers of Chinese did not seem to match exactly with other groups in aspects such as age and educational background. This is because it is virtually impossible to recruit entirely and completely monolingual Chinese native speakers who are also educated to university level. Efforts have been made to ensure that the technical school students recruited have only basic to lower knowledge of English due to the course design in their school.

We followed norms and procedures in experiments reported in Chapters 4 and 5 in aspects of material design, test administration, data coding and data analysis.

6.2 Results

We used *R* and lme4 (Bates *et al.*, 2012) to perform two linear mixed effects analyses on the dependent variables of a. the decision strategy (i.e. preferences), and b. the RT.

6.2.1 *Mean proportion of Manner-matches and Path-matches across* 4 *participant groups*

Participants' choices were categorized into two types: Manner-match and Path-match. Figure 5, below, represents the mean proportion of Manner- and Path-matches across four groups.

We used linear mixed-effects (LME) modelling via restricted maximum likelihood for repeated-measures analyses (Judd et al., 2012). As random effect, we had intercepts representing participant number and stimulus items. For preferences, participants groups (i.e. four levels) and event type [i.e. caused motion(CM) vs. voluntary motion (VM)] were entered as a fixed-effect factor. To assess the validity of the mixed effects analyses, we performed likelihood ratio tests comparing the models with fixed effects to the null models with only the random effects. We rejected results in which the model including fixed effects did not differ significantly from the null model.

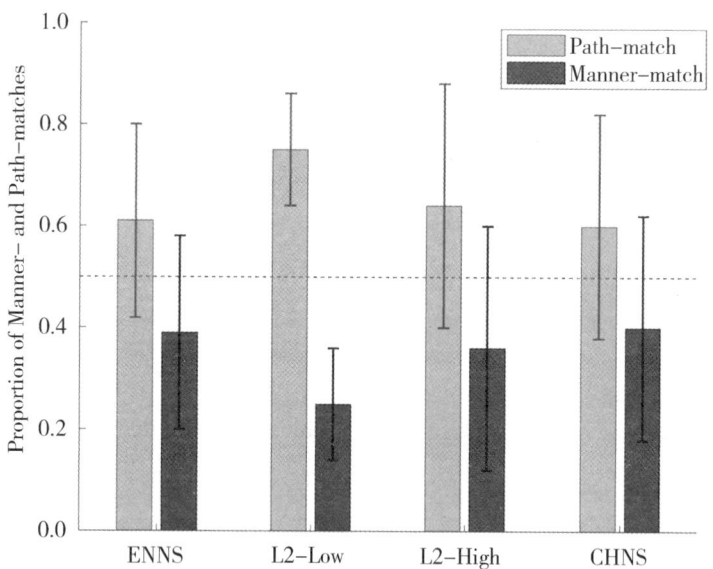

Figure 5 Mean proportion of Path-matches and Manner-matches across 4 groups

error bars represent SDs

Chapter 6 Conceptualising Motion Events in L2 Chinese Learners (Experiment 3)

Our analysis revealed a main effect of participant group [χ^2 (3) =10.89, p =0.01] only. There was no main effect of event type [$\chi^2(1)$ =0.46, p =0.50], nor any interaction between participant group and event type (χ^2 =0.67, df =3, ns). To further test this observation, we examined, for each participant group, if the proportion of preferences for the Path-match (which was complementary with that for the Manner-match) differed significantly from the chance level (50%). We conducted one-sample t tests (against 0.5) for each participant group. The results revealed that the proportion for the Path-match was significantly above the chance level among all groups: ENNS [M =0.61; SD =0.19; t (31) =3.16, p <0.01], L2-Low [M =0.75; SD =0.11; t (27) = 11.74, p <0.001], L2-High [M =0.64; SD =0.24; t (22) =2.76, p =0.01], and CHNS [M =0.60; SD =0.22; t (31) =2.72, p = 0.01][①].

We proceeded to examine how the preferences differed significantly across the four participant groups (ENNS, L2-Low, L2-High and CHNS). Mixed model logistic regression was carried out using R (version 3.0.3) with glmer function and the package lmerTest to obtain parameter estimates. The overt choice of participants was coded as a binomial dependent variable: the preference for the Path-match was coded as '1' and that for the Manner-match was coded as '0'. It was found that the group of L2-Low chose Path-matches significantly more frequently than participants from the other three groups (vs. ENNS [b = - 0.90,

---

① The abbreviations for participant groups are as follows: CHNS = Chinese monolingual speakers; ENNS = English monolingual speakers; L2-Low = L2 learners of Chinese with low proficiency; L2-High = L2 learners of Chinese with high proficiency.

SE =0.31, t = −2.95, p <0.01]; vs. L2-High [b = −0.64, SE = 0.33, t = −1.92, p =0.05]; vs. CHNS [b = −0.91, SE =0.31, t = −2.99, p <0.01]).

These results indicate that participants across groups preferred the Path-match (M =0.65, SD =0.20) over the Manner-match (t = 7.88, df =114, p <0.001), and this tendency could be particularly strong in certain population (e.g. L2-Low). Such a preference for the Path-match remained systematic between VM (M =0.63, SD =0.23) and CM situations (M =0.67, SD =0.20).

6.2.2 The proportion of Path-matches across stimulus items

Further investigations were conducted to see how systematic the preference for the Path-match was across individual test items. Figure 6, below, presents the mean proportion of Path-matches across 32 stimulus items. A visual inspection of the figure showed that the responses to individual items were not uniform.

We used R and lme4 to perform a further linear mixed effects analysis with participant group (ENNS, L2-Low, L2-High, CHNS) as between subjects factors and test item (32) as a within-subjects factor. To assess the validity of the mixed effects analyses, we performed likelihood ratio tests comparing the models with fixed effects to the null models with only the random effects. We rejected results in which the model including fixed effects did not differ significantly from the null model. It was found that there was a significant difference across test items (χ^2 =703.57, df =31, p < 0.001), suggesting that a particular item was viewed as more salient in Manner or in Path. To illustrate, the frequency of the Path-match with item 23 (target: pulling tyre towards rails; alternates: pulling

Chapter 6 Conceptualising Motion Events in L2 Chinese Learners (Experiment 3)

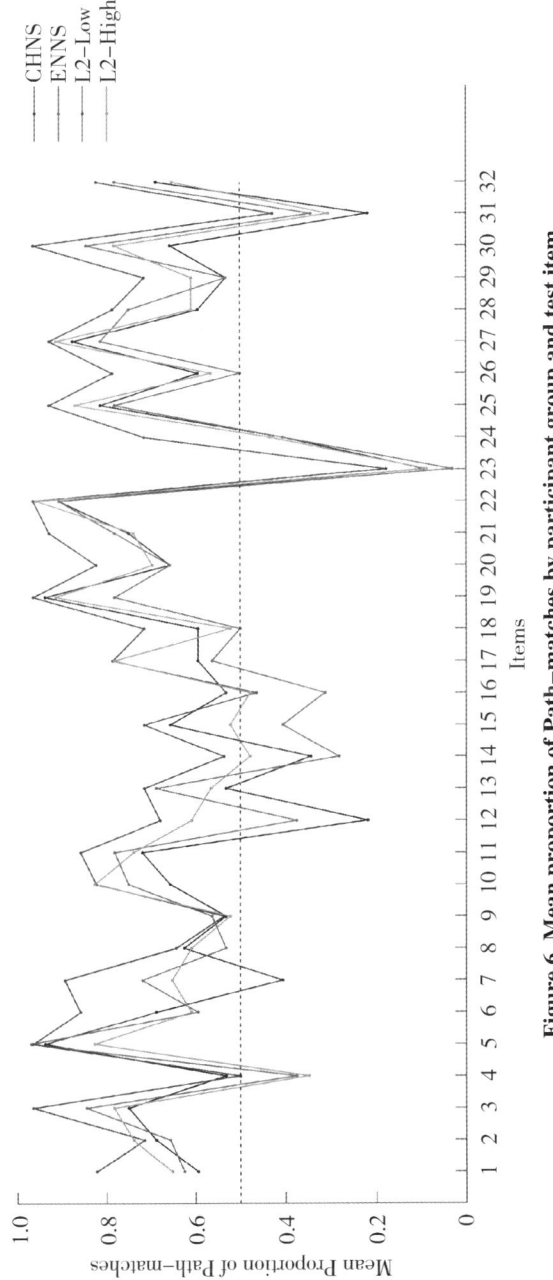

Figure 6 Mean proportion of Path-matches by participant group and test item

tyre *along* rails, *throwing* tyre towards rails) fell below the chance level (50%; i.e., more Manner-matches): $\chi^2(1) = 37.60$, $p < 0.001$, $M = 0.10$, $SD = 0.30$, whereas the frequency of the Path-match with item 5 (target: dragging barrel around table; alternates: dragging barrel *away from* table, *rolling* barrel around table) was significantly above the chance level (i.e. more Path-matches, $\chi^2(1) = 36.00$, $p < 0.001$, $M = 0.90$, $SD = 0.31$. Such findings indicated that apart from a common tendency of preferring the Path-matched video clips, there were certain aspects of the designed items that directed the attention of speakers to either Path or Manner constantly.

6.2.3 RT across 4 participant groups

The RT for a given stimulus was calculated from the onset of alternate videos to the completion of a trial, including a 1 second black screen at the end of each trial. Although the theoretically longest RT could be 6000 ms, participants were actually encouraged to make their decisions as quickly as possible. 12 out of 3636 were null responses to stimuli and were removed from the dataset in the first instance. Further, observations that were standing more than two standard deviations (SD) from the group mean were considered outliers for long RTs and thus excluded from the dataset. 156 such observations were cleaned. Therefore, a total of 168 observations out of a total of 3636 (4.62%) were removed from the RT data, leaving 3468 values for final analysis. The RT data was log-transformed due to its skewed distribution.

Figure 7 (and Table 7), below, represents the mean RT (in ms) to Manner- and Path-matches across 4 groups in the VM condition (error bars represent *SD*s).

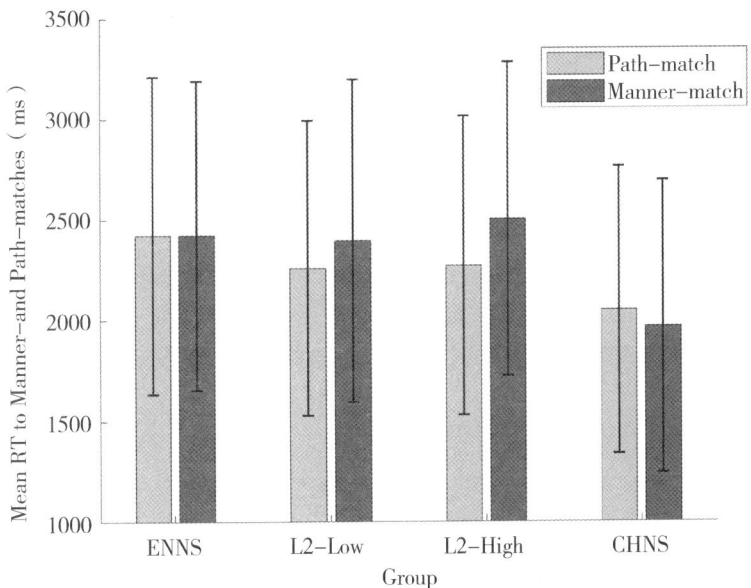

RT to Manner-match: CHNS <ENNS, L2-Low, L2-High, ps <0.01
RT to Path-match: CHNS <ENNS, L2-Low, L2-High, ps <0.01

Figure 7 The mean RT (in ms) to Manner- and Path-matches across participant groups
error bars represent SDs

Table 7 Mean RT (in ms) to stimulus motion scenes in 4 participant groups

Group	Mean overall RT (SD)	Mean RT to Manner-match (SD)	Mean RT to Path-match (SD)
ENNS	2422 (779)	2421 (766)	2422 (788)
L2-Low	2293 (751)	2395 (801)	2260 (732)
L2-High	2354 (761)	2502 (777)	2272 (741)
CHNS	2020 (719)	1968 (726)	2051 (713)

We used *R* and lme4 (Bates *et al.*, 2012) to perform linear mixed effects analyses on the dependent variable of RT. We used linear mixed-effects (LME) modelling via restricted maximum likelihood for repeated-measures analyses (Judd et al., 2012). As random effect, we had intercepts representing participant number and stimuli items. For the RTs, participant group (i.e. ENNS, L2-Low, L2-High, CHNS), event type (voluntary motion, caused motion), and preference (i.e. Path-match, Manner-match) were treated as fixed-effect factors. To assess the validity of the mixed effects analyses, we performed likelihood ratio tests comparing the models with fixed effects to the null models with only the random effects. We rejected results in which the model including fixed effects did not differ significantly from the null model.

Results revealed that the three-way interaction between participant group, event type and preference was not significant, $\chi^2(3) = 0.22, p = 0.22$. The main effect of event type was also not significant, $\chi^2(1) = 0.0023, p = 0.96$. However, the main effect of participant group was significant, $\chi^2(3) = 15.32, p = 0.002$. More importantly, the interaction between participant group and preference showed an expected trend by approaching a level of significance $[\chi^2(3) = 6.53, p = 0.088]$.

Our results revealed, in the first instance, that the overall RT of Chinese monolinguals ($M = 2020, SD = 719$) was significantly shorter than the other three groups: vs. L2-Low ($M = 2293, SD = 751, b = 0.14224, SE = 0.05577, t = 2.551, p = 0.012$); vs. L2-High ($M = 2354, SD = 761, b = 0.1667, SE = 0.05891, t = 2.83, p = 0.0055$), and vs. ENNS ($M = 2422, SD = 779, b = 0.20171, SE = 0.05391, t = 3.742, p = 0.00029$). A closer look at the data suggested that the general high efficiency on the part of Chinese monolingual speakers was actually attributable to their particularly quicker reaction to both Manner- and Path-matches, as compared to English monolingual speakers as well as the other two groups of L2 learners. Thus, we proceed to decompose the interaction effect by looking at group differences in RTs in Path- vs. Manner-matched conditions, respectively. For the Manner-matched condition, participants in the CHNS group responded significantly faster (M =1968, SD =726) than those in the other three groups, i.e. ENNS: M =2421, SD =766, b =0.20924, SE =0.0554, t =3.777, p <0.001; L2-High: M = 2502, SD =777, b =0.20453, SE =0.06193, t =3.303, p <0.01; L2-Low: M =2395, SD =801, b =0.20454, SE =0.05886, t = 3.475, p <0.001. No other significant differences were detected between any other two groups.

For the Path-matched condition, participants in the group of CHNS (M =2051, SD =713) also responded faster as compared to those in all the other three groups (vs. ENNS: M =2422, SD =788, b =0.20155, SE =0.05678, t =3.55, p <0.001; vs. L2-High: M = 2272, SD =741, b =0.16147, SE =0.06209, t =2.601, p =0.0106; vs. L2-Low, M =2260, SD =732, b =0.11508, SE =0.05828, t = 1.975, p =0.0509). No other significant differences were reported between any other two groups.

6.3 Discussion of the results

In this chapter, we focused on the English learners of Chinese at different proficiencies with the aim of revealing: a) how participants judge the similarity between motion video clips, Manner-similarity or Path-similarity; whether, and how, their judgment is affected by factors such as motion event typology (satellite-framed English vs. equipollently-framed Chinese) and proficiency level of L2 learners (advanced vs. low-intermediate); and b) compared to the explicit measurement of decision strategies (i.e. A or B choices in judgment), whether, and how, the pattern of response latency (as measured by

RT) varies with participant group.

Our main findings are twofold. First of all, in terms of choices, all participants prefer the Path-match over the Manner-match, irrespective of their learner type (i.e. monolinguals vs. L2 learners). This shared tendency for the Path-match remains systematic across event type (i.e. spontaneous vs. provoked). Further, there was an absence of developmental progression across proficiencies in L2 Chinese learners, suggesting that factors such as exposure to L2 and age of L2 acquisition have virtually no impact on participants' decision strategy in motion event judgment. Secondly, as regards the RT pattern, there was a strong inclination towards an interaction effect of participant group and preference. Specifically, the overall RT on the part of Chinese monolinguals was significantly shorter than that in English monolinguals, as well as the two learner groups. Further, after decomposing the interaction effect along the Manner- vs. Path-matched dimensions, it was found that Chinese monolinguals were particularly efficient in judging both Manner-matched scenes and Path-match scenes, the differences in RT between these two dimensions were trivial.

The first set of findings regarding preferences is highly consistent with previous studies utilizing the same stimulus items and similar research methodologies. It further confirms that the predominating tendency towards Path-matches in motion event cognition is irrespective of event type (i.e. VM and CM) and learner type (L2 English learners and L2 Chinese learners).

As regards the performance of L2 Chinese learners, they did not demonstrate clear signs of restructuring their motion event cognition pattern, even with increasing language proficiency. Such recalibration of one's linguistic categories, perspectives and frames of reference is actually documented in previous findings, particularly in relation to

Chapter 6 Conceptualising Motion Events in L2 Chinese Learners (Experiment 3)

advanced L2 learners and in domains such as colour perception and object categorisation (Pavlenko, 2011: 247). The reasons that our L2 participants fail to diverge from their L1 thinking pattern and resemble that of the L2 speakers may be multiple. Several contributing forces, however, deserve our attention. Most of our L2 participants begin to study Chinese after adolescence with a limited amount of L2 exposure (i.e. less than 4 years on average). Although an immersion in the (extra)linguistic context of Chinese language and Chinese culture and the frequency of Chinese use may be advantages in acquisition for our L2 learners, the amount and the type of conceptual adjustment seem challenging. The English learners of Chinese need to incorporate a new pattern of motion event cognition (i.e. Path salience) into their L1 thinking mode and further, internalise such a new pattern absent in their L1. No target-like performance will appear unless this process of internalisation is complete. This, at least partly, explains why even advanced learners of Chinese in our study still behave like monolingual speakers of their L1 in the pattern of response latency.

Last but not least, the findings in this chapter suggest a main effect of test item in the proportion of Path-matches. A further look at the data indicates that language-specific pattern of motion expression might have an impact on participants' (monolingual speakers in particular) motion event cognition. To give an example, stimulus item 15 demonstrates a target scene of a boy dragging a toy car across a small icy lake. The two alternates depict the same boy dragging a toy car around the icy lake (i.e. Path change) and sliding a toy car across the icy lake (Manner change), respectively. Statistical analyses show that regarding this item, the mean proportion of Path-matches is significantly higher in Chinese monolinguals ($M = 0.66$, $SD = 0.48$) than in their English counterparts ($M = 0.41$, $SD = 0.50$;

$b = 0.25$, SE $= 0.12$, $t = 2.05$, $p < 0.05$). The most important feature of design in item 15 is that it involves a particular Path, i. e., a Path that is parallel to the Ground of motion: *around*. In some other cases, the Path involves deixis such as *towards* and *away from*. In Chinese, these two types of Path require periphrastic means for linguistic expression. Instead of using 'spatial locatives' (i.e. directional complements) immediately after the main verb (e.g. *la* 1 *guo* 4 'drag-across', *gun* 3 *shang* 4 'roll-up'), the periphrastic means of expression prefixes spatial locatives such as *wei* 2 'around' and *chao* 2 'towards', placing them in front of the main verb and suffixing them with a durative marker *zhe* (e.g. 'The boy, *around* the lake, was dragging a toy car'; 'He, *towards* the escalator, was rolling a sack'). In a sense, *towards* and *around* are treated very much like verbs in Chinese rather than prepositions, reflecting the fact that these two constituents were once full verbs in Archaic Chinese, which was typically verb-framed (Peyraube, 2006). Such important differences in the expression of Path, such as *around* and *towards* versus those of *up* and *across*, might have some cognitive implications. They might have directed more attention to the Path dimension on the part of Chinese monolinguals and thus prompted them to perceive, and judge, relevant motion scenes on the basis of Path similarity (rather than Manner resemblance).

Chapter 7
General Remarks

The present study aims to investigate the mental conceptualisation of motion events in L1 and L2 learners. It consists of 3 experiments, which compare the cognitive representation of motion in different types of learners and discuss extensively the theoretical implications of such comparisons (i.e. at the end of each individual chapter).

Experiment 1 aims to test whether Chinese-English bilinguals can reconstruct their cognitive pattern in the direction of the target system when judging the similarity between spontaneous motion screens. English main verbs encode Manner of motion only, while Chinese verb compounds express Manner and Path simultaneously. As a result, Chinese monolinguals are predicted to develop a motion cognition pattern highlighting both Manner and Path salience whereas English monolinguals are more likely to be Manner-oriented. The research findings are twofold. First, when assessed by the explicit measure of selection strategies (i.e. either Manner-match or Path-match), both monolingual and bilingual speakers show a general preference for the Path-match, attributable either to the universal Path salience in motion event conceptualisation or to a Whorfian effect nullified by verbal interference. However, when gauged by the implicit measure of processing speed (i.e. RT), the Chinese monolinguals reacted significantly quicker than their English counterparts, particularly in making Path-matched judgments, which is arguably due to the fact that Path is given greater prominence in Chinese than in English. Further, the L2 learners across proficiencies responded significantly more slowly than their monolingual counterparts even at an advanced stage of acquisition, suggesting that the process of conceptual reconstructing, as demonstrated in the particular experimental situation, can be cognitively demanding and needs a longer period of time to complete. In general, these findings reveal a possible effect of language typology on motion event cognition, consistent with a weak version of the linguistic relativity hypothesis.

Experiment 2 proceeds to investigate the conceptualisation of caused motion events in an L2 context. Specifically, it explores whether typological differences between English and Chinese influence how first and second language learners conceptualise caused motion events, as suggested by behavioural evidences. Thus, the performance of Chinese learners of English, at three proficiencies, was compared to that of two groups of monolingual speakers in a triads matching task. The first set of analyses regarding categorisation preferences indicates that participants across groups preferred the Path-matched (rather than Manner-matched) screens. However, the second set of analyses regarding RT suggests, firstly, that English monolingual speakers reacted significantly more quickly in selecting the Manner-matched scenes compared with monolingual speakers of Chinese, who tended to use an approximately equal amount of time in making Manner-matched and Path-matched decisions, a finding that can be arguably mapped onto the typological differences between the two languages. Secondly, the pattern of response latency in low-level L2 learners looked more like that of monolingual speakers of Chinese. Only at intermediate and advanced levels of acquisition did the behavioural pattern of L2 learners become target-like, thus suggesting language-specific constraints from L1 at an early stage of acquisition. Such findings suggest that motion event cognition may be linked to, among other things, the linguistic structure of motion description in particular languages.

Experiment 3 focuses on the L2 Chinese learners across proficiencies in their judgment of motion event similarities. It is found that participants across groups rely more frequently on the criterion of Path-match (rather than Manner-match), irrespective of event type (spontaneous and provoked) and learner type (monolinguals and L2 learners). Further, the analyses of the RT data reveal that Chinese monolinguals reacted significantly more quickly than all other participants, reflecting a possible effect of language typology in which Chinese attaches equal significance to Manner and Path. This helps to foster an approximately equal amount of attention to Manner and Path in Chinese monolinguals and further helps them process these two types of semantic information in a parallel way, thus contributing to the particularly high efficiency of Chinese monolinguals in their similarity judgements.

7.1 Significance of the study

Specific research findings and their implications have been extensively discussed in individual chapters. On the whole, the present study has produced valuable results highlighting the implications of typological constraints for motion event conceptualisation, and has thus provided an important insight into the relationship between language and cognition. Our general findings suggest that the cognitive recalibration of one's L1 thinking pattern may not be as difficult as was traditionally hypothesized. Conceptual restructuring or convergence in L2 learners is possible under given conditions, say, at a high language proficiency level or an involvement of relatively low cognitive load. In addition, the present study may have psycholinguistic implications beyond the particular domain of motion given that it touches upon some other aspects such as the conceptualisation of causality and the online event construal.

It should be highlighted that our findings are drawn from a large database, the scale of which far exceeds that observed in previous studies. Firstly, the study involves monolingual adult speakers as well as Chinese-English bilinguals across three proficiencies, making a total of about 500 participants overall. It also includes 96 experimental stimuli, which vary systematically along several important dimensions (e.g. voluntary motion versus provoked motion, Manner and Path salience versus Manner salience alone, vertical Path versus Path of deixis, etc.). Experimental testing of this large and varied set of stimuli in both Chinese and English leads to the collection of a set of particularly rich data in both languages, which comprised nearly 15000 target responses, all being analysed by advanced psycholinguistic tools (e.g. three-way mixed ANOVA, mixed models analysis).

Secondly, this study looks at two types of motion contexts, voluntary motion and caused motion, which, together, incorporate the most complete set of semantic ingredients for motion (i.e. Figure, Ground, Motion, Manner, Path and Cause), thus allowing us to draw comparisons between English and Chinese, a language with intriguing typological properties in great need of exploration. The comparison between two languages with relatively close typological distance (rather than opposing typological features) is particularly meaningful in the sense that it allows us to test the 'degree of differences' in one's thinking pattern and behavioural pattern, as compared to the traditional practice of focusing on the existence or absence of any differences (e.g. A or B choices in similarity judgment or categorisation task).

Thirdly, the current study employs a symmetrical design where the two languages of Chinese and English appear both as the L1 and as the L2 of participants. It merits mentioning that very few studies have implemented such a design due to various limitations. Thus, the present study enables us to examine the directionality (i.e. from Chinese to English or vice versa) and the type of required conceptual adjustment in a bilingual mind (e.g. suppression of an already existing conceptual pattern or incorporation of a new thinking mode), which helps to better predict the progress of conceptual restructuring that takes place in the process of additional language learning.

7.2 Directions for future research

There are several desired lines of investigation for future research. First of all, as previously commented, the present study involves two languages that are only partially different from (or similar to) each other. Given that there are no differences attested in terms of preferences, irrespective of participant group, event type and learner type, it might be better for future studies to include one more type of language for comparison, that is, a typical verb-framed language such as Spanish. This will help to exclude the possibility that an absence of significant differences in participants' decision strategy (i.e. a shared tendency for Path-matches) is due to the 'too close' typological distance between English and Chinese, which fails to bring out the otherwise existing differences in selection patterns across groups of participants.

As regards testing conditions, the present study aims to be truly nonlinguistic by utilizing either a number shadowing technique in which a sequence of random digits are broadcasted to participants during the testing phase, or a 'counting back' task in which participants are asked to count backwards from 100 to 1. The purpose of such techniques is to avoid the loophole of logical circularity, thus guaranteeing that there are no verbal interferences with participants' cognitive processes. Future research is encouraged to include two more testing conditions in order to illustrate, more clearly, any language effect (if any) on cognition under varied circumstances: a) a verbal encoding condition in which participants are invited to linguistically describe the motion events immediately prior to the similarity judgment task, and b) a covert encoding condition in which no verbal interferences are present and participants are free to subconsciously describe motion events whilst judging the similarity between these events. The former condition provides clear language signals that participants may utilize in their subsequent judgment and the latter condition allows language signals to be present in the immediate context of experiment (though not ostensively, i.e. in the subconsciousness of participants). A comparison of research findings under three testing conditions (i.e. number shadowing, verbal encoding and covert encoding) will help to reveal how language is used in online cognitive process, viz., as a tool for event interpretation (as in the verbal encoding circumstance) or as a strategy available to aid event construal (as in the covert encoding condition).

  Last but not least, as far as the stimulus design is concerned, the present study encourages participants to base their judgments on the overall similarity of actions between motion scenes. We have used an implicit measurement of RT, apart from an explicit measurement of preference, to assess the conceptual pattern of participants. In the particular set-up of the current experiment, the RT is calculated from

Chapter 7   General Remarks

the onset of alternate video clips in each triad. In a sense, such kind of RT is more related to the processing of the whole event rather than to the processing of Manner or Path as a separate dimension. The interpretability of the RTs as evidence of processing Manner or Path dimensions can be improved in future experiments by guaranteeing a consistency between stimulus items as to when the critical difference between the Path and Manner alternates becomes manifest (i.e. the frames showing either the Manner or the Path has been changed).

References

Allen, S., Ozyurek, A., & Kita, S. (2007). Language-specific and universal influences in children's syntactic packaging of Manner and Path: A comparison of English, Japanese, and Turkish. *Cognition*, 102 (1), 16-48.

Athanasopoulos, P. (2009). Cognitive representation of colour in bilinguals: The case of Greek blues. *Bilingualism*, 12, 83-95.

Athanasopoulos, P., & Bylund, E. (2013). Does grammatical aspect affect motion event cognition? A cross-linguistic comparison of English and Swedish speakers. *Cognitive Science*, 37, 286-309.

Athanasopoulos, P., Bylund, E., Monteromelis, G., Damjanovic, L., Schartner, A., & Kibbe, A. (2015a). Two languages, two minds: Flexible cognitive processing driven by language of operation. *Psychological Science*, 26 (4), 518.

Athanasopoulos, P., Damjanovic, L., Burnand, J., & Bylund, E. (2015b). Learning to think in a second language: Effects of proficiency and length of exposure in English learners of German. *Modern Language Journal*, 99, 138-153.

Bates, D., Maechler, M., and Bolker, B. (2012). lme4: Linear mixed-effects models using S4 classes.

Beavers, J., Levin, B., & Tham, S. W. (2010). The typology of motion expressions revisited. *Journal of Linguistics*, 46 (2), 331-377.

Berman, R., & Slobin, D. I. (1994). *Relating Events in Narrative: A Crosslinguistic Developmental Study*. Hillsdale, NJ: Lawrence Erlbaum Associates.

References

Berthele, R. (2004). The typology of motion and posture verbs: A variationist account. In B. Kortmann (Ed.), *Dialectology Meets Typology: Dialect Grammar from a Cross-Linguistic Perspective* (93-126). Berlin/New York: Mouton de Gruyter.

Bialystok, E. (2009). Bilingualism: The good, the bad, and the indifferent. *Bilingualism: Language and Cognition*, 12 (1), 3-11.

Bohnemeyer, J., Eisenbeiss, S. & Narasimhan, B. (2004). Manner and path in non-linguistic cognition. Paper presented at the International Conference on Language, Culture & Mind, University of Portsmouth, 18-20 July.

Boroditsky, L. (2001). Does language shape thought? Mandarin and English speakers' conceptions of time. *Cognitive Psychology*, 43. 1-22.

Bowerman, M. (1988). The child's expression of meaning: Expanding relationships among lexicon, syntax, and morphology. In M. B. Franklin & S. S. Barten (Eds.), *Child Language: A Reader* (106-107). New York, Oxford: Oxford University Press.

Bowerman, M. (1994). From universal to language-specific in early grammatical development. *Philosophical Transactions of the Royal Society of London* B, 346, 37-45.

Bowerman, M. (1996). The origins of children's spatial semantic categories: Cognitive versus linguistic determinants. In J. Gumperz & S. Levinson (Eds.), *Rethinking Linguistic Relativity* (145-176). Cambridge: Cambridge University Press.

Bowerman, M. (1999). Learning how to structure space for language: A crosslinguistic perspective. In P. M. Bloom & L. Peterson (Eds.), *Language and Space* (385-436). Cambridge, MA: MIT Press.

Bowerman, M. & Choi, S. (2001). Shaping meanings for language: Universal and language-specific in the acquisition of spatial semantic categories. In M. Bowerman & S. C. Levinson (Eds.), *Language Acquisition and Conceptual Development* (475-511). Cambridge: Cambridge University Press.

Bowerman, M. & Choi, S. (2003). Space under construction: Language-specific categorisation in first language acquisition. In D. Gentner & S. Goldin-Meadow (Eds.), *Language in Mind: Advances in the Study of Language and Thought* (387-427). Cambridge, MA: MIT Press.

Brown, A., & Gullberg, M. (2010). Changes in encoding of PATH of motion in a first language during acquisition of a second language. *Cognitive Linguistics*, 21, 263-286.

Brown, P. (2004). Position and motion in Tzeltal frog stories: The acquisition of narrative style. In S. Stromqvist & L. Verhoeven (Eds.), *Relating Events in Narrative: Crosslinguistic and Crosscontextual Perspectives* (37-58). Mahwath, N. J. : Earlbaum.

Bylund, E., & Athanasopoulos, P. (2014). Linguistic relativity in SLA: Toward a new research program. *Language Learning*, 64, 952-985.

Bylund, E., Athanasopoulos, P., & Oostendorp, M. (2013). Motion event cognition and grammatical aspect: Evidence from afrikaans. *Linguistics*, 51 (5), 929-955.

Cadierno, T. (2004). Expressing motion events in a second language: A cognitive typological perspective. In M. Achard & S. Niemeier (Eds.), *Cognitive Linguistics, Second Language Acquisition, and Foreign Language Teaching* (13-49). Berlin: Mouton de Gruyter.

Cadierno, T. (2008). Learning to talk about motion in a foreign language. In P. Robinson, & N. C. Ellis (Eds.), *Handbook of Cognitive Linguistics and Second Language Acquisition* (239-275). New York & London: Routledge.

Cadierno, T. (2010). Motion in Danish as a second language: Does

References

the learner's L1 make a difference? In Z. H. Han, & T. Cadierno (Eds.), *Linguistic Relativity in SLA: Thinking for Speaking* (1-33). Clevedon: Multilingual Matters.

Cadierno, T., & Ruiz, L. (2006). Motion events in Spanish L2 acquisition. *Annual Review of Cognitive Linguistics*, 4, 183-216.

Chao, Y. R. (1968). *A Grammar of Spoken Chinese*. Berkeley, CA: University of California.

Chen, J., & Ai, R. (2009). Encoding motion and state change in L2 Mandarin. In Y. Xiao (Ed.), *Proceedings of the 21st North American Conference on Chinese Linguistics* (NACCL-21) Volume 1 (149-164). Smithfield, RI: Bryant University.

Chen, L. (2005). The acquisition and use of motion event expressions in Chinese. Unpublished doctoral dissertation. University of Louisiana, Lafayette, LA.

Chen, L., & Guo, J. (2009). Motion events in Chinese novels: Evidence for an equivalently-framed language. *Journal of Pragmatics*, 41, 1749-1766.

Choi, S., & Bowerman, M. (1991). Learning to express motion events in English and Korean: The influence of language-specific lexicalisation patterns. *Cognition*, 41, 83-121.

Chu, C. Z. (2009). Path of motion: Conceptual structure and representation in Chinese. In Z. Xing (Ed.), *Studies of Chinese Linguistics: Functional Approaches* (65-73). Hong Kong: Hong Kong University Press.

Clark, H. H. (1973). Space, time, semantics, and the child. In T. Moore (Ed.), *Cognitive Development and the Acquisition of Language* (27-63). New York: Academic Press.

Clark, H. H., & Chase, W. G. (1972). On the process of comparing sentences against pictures. *Cognitive Psychology*, 3, 472-517.

Collins, A. M., & Quillian, M. R. (1969). Retrieval time from semantic memory. *Journal of Verbal Learning and Verbal Behaviour*, 8, 240-247.

Cook, V., & Bassetti, B. (2011). *Language and Cognition*. New York, NY: Psychology Press.

Costa, A., Hernandez, M., & Sebastian-Galles, N. (2008). Bilingualism aids conflict resolution: Evidence from the ANT task. *Cognition*, 106 (1), 59-86.

Croft, W., Baredal, J., Hollmann, W., Sotirova, V., & Taoka, C. (2002). Revising Talmy's typological classification of complex events. Paper read at the Annual Meeting of the Linguistic Society of America. Atlanta, January 2002.

Czechowska, N., & Ewert, A. (2011). Perception of motion by Polish-English bilinguals. In V. Cook & B. Bassetti (Eds.), *Language and Cognition* (287-314). New York: Psychology Press.

Daller, M. H., Treers-Daller, J., & Furman, R. (2011). Transfer of conceptualisation patterns in bilinguals: The construal of motion events in Turkish and German. *Bilingualism*, 14, 95-119.

Farwell, C. (1977). The primacy of "goal" in the child's description of motion and location. *Papers and Reports on Child Language Development*, 16, 126-133.

Fernald, A., Zangl, R., Portillo, A. L. & Marchman, V. A. (2008). Looking while listening: Using eye movements to monitor spoken language comprehension by infants and young children. In I. A. Sekerina, E. M. Fernandez & H. Clahsen (Eds.), *Developmental Psycholinguistics: On-line Methods in Childrenp's Language Processing* (97-135). Amsterdam: John Benjamins.

Filipovic, L. (2011). Speaking and remembering in one or two languages: Bilingual vs. monolingual lexicalisation and memory for motion events. *International Journal of Bilingualism*, 15, 466-485.

Filipovic, L., & Jaszczolt, K. (Eds.). (2012). *Space and Time in*

Languages and Cultures : Linguistic Diversity. London: John Benjamins.

Flecken, M., Athanasopoulos, P., Kuipers, J. R., & Thierry, G. (2015). On the road to somewhere: Brain potentials reflect language effects on motion event perception. *Cognition*, 141, 41-51.

Flecken, M., von Stutterheim, C., & Carroll, M. (2014). Grammatical aspect influences motion event perception: Findings from a cross-linguistic nonverbal recognition task. *Language and Cognition*, 6, 45-78.

Gao, H. (2001). Notions of motion and contact for physical contact verbs. In A. Holmer, J. Svantesson & A. Viberg (Eds.), *Proceedings of the 18th Scandinavian Conference of Linguistics*, vol. 2 (193-209). Lund: University of Lund.

Gennari, S., Sloman, S., Malt, B., & Fitch, W. (2002). Motion events in language and cognition. *Cognition*, 83, 49-79.

Gullberg, M. (2011). Language-specific encoding of placement events in gestures. In J. Bohnemeyer & E. Pederson (Eds.), *Event representation in Language and Cognition* (166-188). Cambridge, MA: Cambridge University Press.

Gullberg, M., Hendriks, H., & Hickmann, M. (2008). Learning to talk and gesture about motion in French. *First Language*, 28/2, 200-236.

Helm-Estabrooks, N. (2004). The problem of perseveration. *Seminars in Speech and Language*, 25, 289-290.

Hendriks, H., & Hickmann, M. (2011). Space in second language acquisition. In V. Cook, & B. Bassetti (Eds.), *Language and Bilingual Cognition* (315-339). Hove: Psychology Press.

Hendriks, H., Hickmann, M., & Demagny, A. C. (2008). How English native speakers learn to express caused motion in English and French. *Acquisition et Interaction en Langue étrangère*, 27, 15-

41. Hendriks, H., Ji, Y., & Hickmann, M. (2008). Typological issues regarding the expression of caused motion: Chinese, English and French. In M. Brala (Ed.), *Space and Time in Language and Literature* (1-15). Cambridge, UK: Cambridge Scholars Press.

Hickmann, M. (2003). *Children's Discourse: Person, Space and Time across Languages.* Cambridge: Cambridge University Press.

Hickmann, M. (2006). The relativity of motion in first language acquisition. In M. Hickmann & S. Robert (Eds.), *Space in Languages: Linguistic Systems and Cognitive Categories* (281-308). Amsterdam: John Benjamins Publishing Company.

Hickmann, M., Hendriks, H., & Champaud, C. (2009). Typological constraints on motion in French and English child language. In J. Guo, E. Lieven, S. Ervin-Tripp, N. Budwig, S. Ozcaliskan & K. Nakamura (Eds.), *Crosslinguistic Approaches to the Psychology of Language: Research in the Tradition of Dan Isaac Slobin* (209-224). New York: Psychology Press.

Hohenstein, J. (2005). Language-related motion event similarities in English- and Spanish-speaking children. *Journal of Cognitive Development*, 6, 403-425.

Hohenstein, J., Eisenberg, A., & Naigles, L. (2006). Is he floating across or crossing afloat? Cross-influence of L1 and L2 in Spanish-English bilingual adults. *Bilingualism: Language and Cognition*, 9, 249-261.

Hunt, E., & Agnoli, F. (1991). The Whorfian hypothesis: A cognitive psychology perspective. *Psychological Review*, 98 (3), 377-389.

Hunt, E., & Banaji, M. (1988). The Whorfian Hypothesis revisited: A cognitive science view of linguistic and cultural effects on thought. In J. Berry, S. Irvine & E. Hunt (Eds.), *Indigenous*

Cognition: *Functioning in Cultural Context* (57-84). Dordrecht, The Netherlands: Martinus Nijhoff.

Iacobini, C. & Masini, F. (2006). The emergence of verb-particle constructions in Italian locative and actional meanings. *Morphology*, 16, 155-188.

Ibarretxe-Antunano, I. (2012). Placement and removal events in Basque and Spanish. In A. Kopecka & B. Narasimhan (Eds.), *Events of "Putting" and "Taking"*: *A crosslinguistic perspective* (123-144). Amsterdam & Philadelphia: John Benjamins.

Jackendoff, R. (1996). The architecture of the linguistic-spatial interface. In P. Bloom, M. Peterson, L. Nadel & M. Garrett (Eds.), *Language and Space* (1-30). Cambridge, MA: MIT Press.

Johnston, J. R. (1988). Children's verbal representation of spatial location. In J. Stiles-Davis, M. Kritchevsky & U. Bellugi (Eds.), *Spatial Cognition*: *Brain Bases and Development* (195-205). Hillsdale, NJ: Lawrence Erlbaum.

Johnston, J. R. & Slobin, D. I. (1979). The development of locative expressions in English, Italian, Serbo-Croatian and Turkish. *Journal of Child Language*, 6, 529-545.

Ji, Y. (2014). *The Expression of Motion Events*: *Typological and Developmental Perspectives*. Beijing: China Social Sciences Press.

Ji, Y. (2017). Motion event similarity judgments in one or two languages: An exploration of monolingual speakers of English and Chinese vs. L2 learners of English. *Frontiers in Psychology-Language Sciences*, 8, 909. doi: 10.3389/fpsyg.2017.00909.

Ji, Y. (2019). Cognitive representation of spontaneous motion in a second language: An exploration of Chinese learners of English. *Frontiers in Psychology-Cognition*. doi: 10.3389/fpsyg.2019.02706.

Ji, Y. (2021). The acquisition of Chinese RVCs in motion event expressions. *Journal of Shenzhen University (Humanities and Social Sciences Edition)*, 38 (6).

Ji, Y., Hendriks, H., & Hickmann, M. (2011a). How children express caused motion events in Chinese and English: Universal and language-specific influences. *Lingua*, 121, 1796-1819.

Ji, Y., Hendriks, H., & Hickmann, M. (2011b). The expression of caused motion events in Chinese and in English: Some typological issues. *Linguistics*, 49 (5), 1041-1076.

Ji, Y., Hendriks, H., & Hickmann, M. (2011c). Children's expression of voluntary motion events in English and Chinese. *Journal of Foreign Languages*, 34 (4), 2-20.

Ji, Y., & Hohenstein, J. (2014a). The syntactic packaging of caused motion components in a second language: English learners of Chinese. *Lingua*, 140, 100-116.

Ji, Y., & Hohenstein, J. (2014b). The expression of caused motion by adult Chinese learners of English. *Language and Cognition*, 6, 427-461.

Ji, Y., & Hohenstein, J. (2018). English and Chinese children's motion event similarity judgments. *Cognitive Linguistics*, Vol. 29 (1), 45-76.

Jin, K. (2020). Learning motion expressions in another language: Practice from Korean learners of Chinese. Unpublished MA thesis. Shenzhen University, Shenzhen, Guangdong Province.

Kersten, A. W., Meissner, C. A., Lechuga, J., Schwartz, B. L., Albrechtsen, J. S., & Iglesias, A. (2010). English speakers attend more strongly than Spanish speakers to manner of motion when classifying novel objects and events. *Journal of Experimental Psychology: General*, 139 (4), 638-653.

Kharkhurin, A. V. (2010). Bilingual verbal and nonverbal creative behaviour. *International Journal of Bilingualism*, 14 (2), 211-226.

Kopecka, A. (2006). The semantic structure of motion verbs in

French: Typological perspectives. In M. Hickmann, & S. Robert (Eds.), *Space in Languages: Linguistic Systems and Cognitive Categories* (83-101). Amsterdam: John Benjamins.

Lai, V. T., & Narasimhan, B. (2008). Verb representation and thinking-for-speaking effects in Spanish-English bilinguals. In D. Almeida & C. Manouilidou (Eds.), *Cognitive Science Perspectives on Verb Representation and Processing* (235-256). New York, NY: Springer.

Landau, B., & Lakusta, L. (2006). Spatial language and spatial representation: Autonomy and interaction. In M. Hickmann & S. Roberts (Eds.), *Space in Languages: Linguistic Systems and Cognitive Categories* (309-333). Amsterdam: John Benjamins.

Landau, B. & Zukowski, A. (2003). Objects, motions, and paths: Spatial language in children with Williams syndrome. *Developmental Neuropsychology (Special Issue: Williams Syndrome)*, 23/1-2, 105-137.

Langacker, R. (2008). *Cognitive Grammar*. Oxford: Oxford University Press.

Levinson, S. C. (2003). *Space in Language and Cognition: Explorations in Cognitive Diversity*. Cambridge: Cambridge University Press.

Li, P., Bates, E., & Macwhinney, B. (1993). Processing a language without inflections: A reaction time study of sentence interpretation in Chinese. *Journal of Memory and Language*, 32, 169-192.

Li, Y. F. (1990). On V-V compounds in Mandarin. *Natural Language and Linguistic Theory*, 8, 177-207.

Lucy, J. (1992). *Grammatical Categories and Cognition*. Cambridge: Cambridge University Press.

Lupyan, G. (2012). Linguistically modulated perception and cognition: The label-feedback hypothesis. *Frontiers in Psychology*,

3, 54. doi:10.3389/fpsyg.2012.00054.
Marotta, G., & Meini, L. (2012). Spatial prepositions in Italian L2: Universal and language-specific principles. In L. Filipovic, & K. Jaszczolt (Eds.), *Space and Time in Languages and Cultures: Linguistic Diversity* (289-324). London: John Benjamins.
Montero-Melis, G., & Bylund, E. (2016). Getting the ball rolling: The cross-linguistic conceptualisation of caused motion. *Language and Cognition*, 1, 1-27.
Montero-Melis, G., Jaeger, T. F., Bylund, E. (2016). Thinking is modulated by recent linguistic experience: Second language priming affects perceived event similarity. *Language Learning*, 66 (3), 636-665.
Muller, N. (1998). Transfer in bilingual first language acquisition. *Bilingualism: Language and Cognition*, 1, 151-171.
Naigles, L., & Terrazas, P. (1998). Motion verb generalisations in English and Spanish: Influences of language and syntax. *Psychological Science*, 9, 363-369.
Navarro, S., & Nicoladis, E. (2005). Describing motion events in adult L2 Spanish narratives. In D. Eddington (Ed.), *Selected Proceedings of the 6th Conference on the Acquisition of Spanish and Portuguese as First and Second Languages* (102-107). Somerville, MA: Cascadilla Proceedings Project.
Papafragou, A., Hulbert, J., & Trueswell, J. (2008). Does language guide event perception? Evidence from eye movements. *Cognition*, 108 (1), 155-184.
Papafragou, A., Massey, C., & Gleitman, L. (2002). Shake, rattle, 'n' roll: The representation of motion in language and cognition. *Cognition*, 84, 189-219.
Pavlenko, A. (2011). *Thinking and Speaking in Two Languages*. Bristol: Multilingual Matters.

Peyraube, A. (2006). Motion events in Chinese: A diachronic study of directional complements. In M. Hickmann & S. Robert (Eds.), *Space in Languages: Linguistic Systems and Cognitive Categories* (121-135). Amsterdam: John Benjamins.

Piaget, J., & Inhelder, B. (1956). *The Child's Conception of Space*. London: Routledge & Kegan Paul.

Pruden, S., Hirsh-Pasek, K., Maguire, M., & Meyer, M. (2004). Foundations of verb learning: Infants categorize path and manner in motion events. In A. Brugos, L. Micciulla & C. E. Smith (Eds.), *Proceedings of the 28th Annual Boston University Conference on Language Development* (461-472). Boston, MA: Cascadilla Press.

Regier, T., & Kay, P. (2009). Language, thought, and colour: Whorf was half right. *Trends in Cognitive Science*, 13, 439-446.

Slobin, D. I. (1996). Two ways to travel: Verbs of motion in English and Spanish. In M. Shibatani & S. A. Thompson (Eds.), *Grammatical Constructions: Their Form and Meaning* (195-217). Oxford: Oxford University Press.

Slobin, D. I. (2004). The many ways to search for a frog: Linguistic typology and the expression of motion events. In S. Strömqvist & L. Verhoeven (Eds.), *Relating Events in Narrative, Vol. 2: Typological and Contextual Perspectives* (157-219). Mahwah, NJ: Lawrence Erlbaum Associates.

Soroli, E., & Hickmann, M. (2010). Language and spatial representations in French and in English: Evidence from eye-movements. In G. Marotta, A. Lenci, L. Meini & F. Rovai (Eds.), *Space in Language* (581-597). Pisa: Editrice Testi Scientifici.

Tai, J. (2003). Cognitive relativism: The Resultative construction in Chinese. *Language and Linguistics*, 4/2, 302-316.

Talmy, L. (1985). Lexicalisation patterns: Semantic structure in lexical form. In T. Shopen (Ed.), *Language Typology and Syntactic*

Description, vol. 3 (36-149). Cambridge: Cambridge University Press.

Talmy, L. (1991). Path to realisation: A typology of event conflation. *Berkeley Working Papers in Linguistics*, 480-519.

Talmy, L. (2000). *Toward a Cognitive Semantics*, Vol. 2: *Typology and Process in Concept Structuring*. Cambridge, MA: MIT Press.

Talmy, L. (2009). Main verb properties and equipollent framing. In J. Guo, E. Lieven, & N. Budwig (Eds.), *Crosslinguistic Approaches to the Psychology of Language: Research in the Tradition of Dan Isaac Slobin* (389-402). New York: Psychology Press.

Thierry, G. (2016). Neurolinguistic relativity: How language flexes human perception and cognition. *Language Learning*, 66, 690-713.

Tokowicz, N., & MacWhinney, B. (2005). Implicit and explicit measures of sensitivity to violations in second language grammar: An event-related potential investigation. *Studies in Second Language Acquisition*, 2, 173-204.

Vidakovic, I. (2012). 'He walked up the pole with arms and legs': Typology in second language acquisition. In L. Filipovic, & K. Jaszczolt (Eds.), *Space and Time in Languages and Cultures: Linguistic Diversity* (233-262). London: John Benjamins.

von Stutterheim, C., Andermann, M., Carroll, M., Flecken, M., & Schmiedtová, B. (2012). How grammaticized concepts shape event conceptualisation in language production: Insights from linguistic analysis, eye tracking data, and memory performance. *Linguistics*, 50 (4), 833-867.

Whorf, B. L. (1956). *Language, Thought and Reality*. Cambridge, MA: MIT Press.

Zlatev, J. (2011). From cognitive to integral linguistics and back again. *Intellectica*, 56, 125-147.

Zlatev, J., & Blomberg, J. (2015). Language may indeed influence

References

thought. *Frontiers in Psychology*, 6, 1631.

Zlatev, J., & David, C. (2004). Three ways to travel: Motion event in French, Swedish and Thai. In A. Soares da Silva (Ed.), *Linguagem, Cultura e Cognicao: Estudos de Linguistica Cognitiva*. Volume II (119-142). Coimbra: Almedina.

Zlatev, J., & Yangklang. P. (2004). A third way to travel: The place of Thai in motion event typology. In S. Strömqvist and L. Verhoeven (Eds.), *Relating Events in Narrative: Cross-linguistic and Cross-contextual Perspective* (159-190). Mahwah, NJ: Lawrence Erlbaum.

Appendices

Examples of Illustration and Description of Motion Event Stimuli

A. Voluntary Motion Events

a. Path of verticality (*up*, *down*)

Target: Walking down stairs
Alternates: *Jumping* down stairs/Walking *up* stairs

b. Path of boundary-crossing (*into*, *out of*)

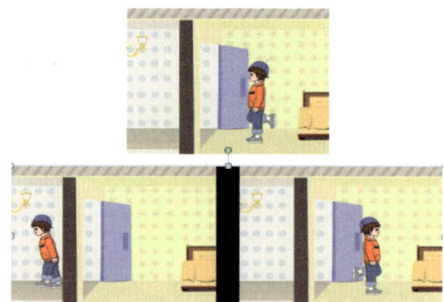

Target: Hopping out of bedroom
Alternates: *Limping* out of bedroom/Hopping *into* bedroom

c. Path of deixis (*towards*, *away from*)

Target: Walking towards house
Alternates: *Jogging* towards house/Walking *out of* house

d. Path parallel to the Ground of motion (*around*, *along*)

Target: Jumping around flower stand
Alternates: *Crawling* around flower stand/Jumping *along* flower stand

B. Caused Motion Events

a. Path of verticality (*up*, *down*)

Target: Kicking balloon up hill
Alternates: Kicking balloon *down* hill/ *Throwing* balloon up hill

b. Path of boundary-crossing (*into*, *out of*)

Target: Kicking ball into paddle
Alternates: Kicking ball *out of* paddle/ *Rolling* ball into paddle

c. Path of deixis (*towards*, *away from*)

Target: Pushing log towards campfire

Alternates: Pushing log *away from* campfire/ *Rolling* log towards campfire

d. Path parallel to the Ground of motion (*around*, *along*)

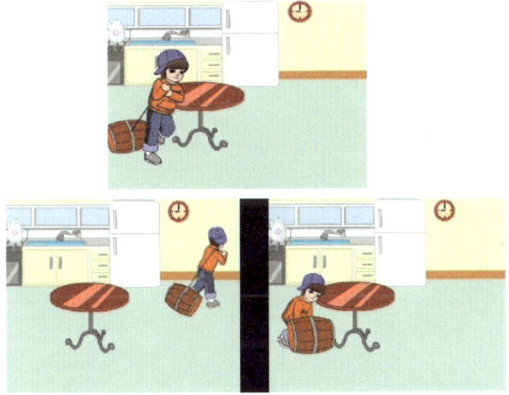

Target: Dragging barrel around table

Alternates: Dragging barrel *away from* table/ *Rolling* barrel *around* table